SIGNPOSTS FOR LIVING

A PSYCHOLOGICAL MANUAL FOR BEING
DR KIRSTEN HUNTER

BOOK 1
**CONTROL YOUR CONSCIOUSNESS –
IN THE DRIVER'S SEAT**

BOOK 2
UNDERSTANDING MYSELF – BE AN EXPERT

BOOK 3
**MINDFULNESS AND STATE OF FLOW –
LIVING WITH PURPOSE AND PASSION**

BOOK 4
**UNDERSTANDING OTHERS –
LOVED ONES TO TRICKY ONES**

BOOK 5
PARENTING – LOVE, PRIDE, APPRENTICESHIP

BOOK 6
NAILING BEING AN ADULT – HAVE THE SKILLS

A MEANINGFUL LIFE

DEVOTE YOURSELF TO:

1. **KNOWING** YOURSELF,

2. **LOVING** OTHERS,

3. **LOVING** YOUR COMMUNITY,

4. **GRATITUDE** FOR THE MOMENT, AND

5. **CREATING SOMETHING** THAT GIVES YOU MEANING AND PURPOSE.

First published 2021 by Kirsten Hunter

Produced by Indie Experts P/L, Australasia
indieexperts.com.au

Copyright © Kirsten Hunter 2021

The moral right of the author to be identified as the author of this work has been asserted.

Except for the purposes of reviewing, no part of this publication may be reproduced or transmitted in any form or by any means, electronic or mechanical, including photocopying, recording or any information storage or retrieval system, without the written permission of the author. Infringers of copyright render themselves viable for prosecution.

Cover design and image by Zach Lawry @ Mates Rates Screen Printing & Design
Edited by Jane Smith @ www.janesmitheditor.com
Internal design by Indie Experts
Typeset in URW DIN by Post Pre-press Group, Brisbane

ISBN 978-1-922742-06-3 (paperback)
ISBN 978-1-922742-07-0 (epub)

Disclaimer: Any information in the book is purely the opinion of the author based on personal experience and should not be taken as business or legal advice. All material is provided for educational purposes only. We recommend to always seek the advice of a qualified professional before making any decision regarding personal and business needs.

To Jon

PREFACE TO THE SERIES

This series of books is actually a conversation that I have had with thousands of people over the last twenty years of clinical psychology work. From approximately 42,000 hours of conversations with clients of all shapes and sizes and from all walks of life, all struggling during their various stages in life, I have learnt so much. When you have the same conversation that many times and you see progress, you see where the value lies. I want to share this conversation with you.

'Signpost for Living' is written out of sheer frustration and exhilaration in equal measure. I have limited hours with my clients. This series of books is the information, across the breadth of 'being human' areas, that I would cover with clients if there was no limit to time. This is my 'ideal situation' series, to share with others how to understand and master ourselves. We are pretty dodgy at being human. We really have very little clue about how we work – we don't fully understand our emotions, our behaviour, our neurology, our physiology – or how to live with purpose, calmness, contentment and joy, with our loved ones and within ourselves. This series covers all of these life-challenge hotspots and things we need to learn about ourselves. If we get support, encouragement, and general guidance in these areas, we can get on track quickly. Life can expand and boom us into more contentment and happiness.

How amazing life is if we allow it to be.

If you get a new puppy, it is wise to put in the time to train it; you can enjoy your pup so much more once it's trained. Your pup becomes easy and fun to walk, reliable on your carpets, and an enjoyable character. This is strangely true for *us* too. By studying our thinking, emotions, behaviour and styles of relating to others – really getting a solid level of self-awareness and having a robust skillset – we can enjoy ourselves and our world so much more. And no, we do *not* need to be puppies to learn new tricks; we can learn as adults, at any stage of life. No excuses here. It is absolutely, profoundly, exasperatingly ridiculous that we do not all learn this information routinely at school. 'How to be human, class 101'. Humans have the code to develop physically, but we need more information to develop psychologically into full adults. Not learning these basic life skills can leave us feeling insecure, disconnected and unsafe.

Life is growth. Life is a work in progress.

This is what these books are about. We do not know everything about 'being human' – far from it – but we do know a fair bit. This knowledge, which comes largely through the profession of psychology, is not, however, common knowledge. And yet it should be. It needs to be. We need a manual for being human, for without it we are driving blind.

This series is based on clinical evidence and sound reasoning. It provides clear, calm direction – not all the answers, but solid signposts. Time to share this knowledge with everyone.

WHAT TO EXPECT IN THE 'SIGNPOSTS FOR LIVING' SERIES

The books in the 'Signposts for Living' series are independent but complementary; by strenghtening and cultivating one area you enhance all of the other areas simultaneously. There is not much point fixing one hole in the boat when the other holes are not receiving attention. This is not a piecemeal series. We need to cover the whole of human functioning. In this series there will be chapters you need, chapters you don't, chapters that talk to you now, chapters that will tap you on the shoulder in your future. The 'Signposts for Living' series is written for everyone: all ages, mums and dads, grandparents, young adults and teenagers finding their way.

The books are broken down to first explore (in Book 1) how controlling your consciousness can help you grab the reins to your nervous system, thoughts and emotions. Relevant side-alleys that are common traps to dodgy thinking are included. We then flesh out your personal issues in Book 2: *Understanding Myself*. The importance of being awake in life and aware of your present moment is celebrated in Book 3, along with the gem of living with purpose and passion in a state of flow. 'Signposts for Living' then broadens in Book 4 to discuss understanding our relationships with our people (the good, the bad and the ugly). The true complexity of parenting is then dissected in Book 5. Finally, the art of nailing being an adult is fleshed out in Book 6, revealing the excitement of reaping the rewards of becoming a thriving mature human.

To make the books as concise and user-friendly as possible, I have avoided references, footnotes and other scholarly tools as much as possible. The goal is for you to be able to access and use this valuable information without feeling bogged down or needing to have specialised, background knowledge. To acknowledge my sources and guide you to delve deeper, if you wish to, I have included 'further reading' lists where relevant at the end of each book.

Welcome to understanding your humanness.

BOOK 4
UNDERSTANDING OTHERS – LOVED ONES TO TRICKY ONES

CONTENTS

CHAPTER 1	CULTIVATE HEALTHY RELATIONSHIPS	1
CHAPTER 2	KINDNESS & COMPASSION – RIPPLE EFFECT	10
CHAPTER 3	WHAT IS LOVE?	14
CHAPTER 4	PARTNER WELL	21
CHAPTER 5	HONEYMOON PHASE: BECOME AN EXPERT ON THEIR 'UGLY'	29
CHAPTER 6	RELATIONSHIP EVOLVING … STAGES	41
CHAPTER 7	POSITIVE – NEGATIVE ATTRIBUTION STYLE	59
CHAPTER 8	HEALTHY RELATIONSHIPS: KNOW THE SKILLS	67
CHAPTER 9	WHAT IS YOUR CAPACITY FOR PERSPECTIVE TAKING?	121
CHAPTER 10	THE FEMALE WANTS TO FEEL HEARD, AND THE MALE WANTS TO GO STRAIGHT TO THE FIX	125
CHAPTER 11	EXPERIENCE SEX, DON'T DO SEX	128
CHAPTER 12	PATIENCE AND TOLERANCE	151
CHAPTER 13	SINGLENESS	154
CHAPTER 14	LONELINESS	156
CHAPTER 15	BREAKING UP HEALTHILY	159
CHAPTER 16	MAKE FORGIVENESS YOUR SUPERPOWER	167
CHAPTER 17	WOMEN RISE BY VALUING OTHER WOMEN	176
CHAPTER 18	SEXISM CONFUSES ME	180
CHAPTER 19	FAMILY	183
CHAPTER 20	LGBTQIA, CELEBRATING OUR INDIVIDUALITY	186

CHAPTER 21	TRICKY TRAUMATIC PEOPLE IN OUR WORLD: PROFILING	188
CHAPTER 22	NARCISSISTIC PERSONALITY DISORDER	191
CHAPTER 23	ABUSE	197
CHAPTER 24	BOUNDARIES ... ASSERTIVENESS	200
CHAPTER 25	FRIENDSHIP	207
CHAPTER 26	MALE AND FEMALE FRIENDSHIPS – DIFFERENT PATHWAYS	215
CHAPTER 27	OUR ROLE MODELS, OUR MENTORS	218
CHAPTER 28	OTHERS ARE GENEROUS	224
CHAPTER 29	SERVE OTHERS, OUR TRIBE, OUR COMMUNITY	226
IN CONCLUSION		230
FURTHER READING		231
ACKNOWLEDGEMENTS		232
ABOUT THE AUTHOR		234

CHAPTER 1
CULTIVATE HEALTHY RELATIONSHIPS

Connection and a sense of belonging keep us healthy. But we are dealing with humans here, and the truth is, if you love you will suffer. And there will be daily struggles, from the trauma caused by toxic people who cross our paths, to the immense grief of losing someone who has shaped our being. So, what to do? The answer: get healthy and strong with our loved ones so that we are growing and building together and not hurting one another. Learn to spot, swerve or manage the truly tricky people in our lives, and be in a stronger place to cope with grief in life when it inevitably comes into our path. How? Let's begin.

> Get healthy and strong with our loved ones
> so that we are growing and building together.

Most of us are social creatures. As relationships can nourish our lives, we need one another to survive. We have endless communication devices to connect us. When we make things happen globally, it is through group endeavours. We look to each other for support and interaction, and to share, learn and grow with one another. We are not islands; it is through our heart connections with loved ones that we find another dimension of meaning. We all want to be taken care of. Smiles, laughter, love and support are perhaps the best things in life, and they all come from nourishing and nourished relationships. As we deepen our connections, we find increasing joy in giving and receiving. Actually, when we give, we are also receiving, as it brings us a sense of joy and satisfaction. It is therefore beyond essential that we nourish, strengthen and support 'our' people. We need to channel our energy towards building stronger and healthier relationships.

There is no substitute for the tenderness of a loved one: not money, not power, not things. We humans rely on soothing from each other. When we are connected and comforted by loved ones, the feel-good hormones **oxytocin** and **endorphins** are released. They work to shut down our threat system and tone down each other's anxiety. Studies have shown that compassion for others and self-compassion both cause the release of these essential comforting hormones. Through compassion, we can help ourselves and each other.

During our life struggles and hard times, it is tenderness that we want, especially as we are facing the end of life. Money might make you comfortable, but it will not hold you. Status is also something to forget about. We want *genuine* connection with people, not one based on impressing each other. If you play this status game, you'll find that those above you will look down on you, and/or those you are lording over will resent and envy you. Status will not give you connection, and on an intimate level, you will be alone.

Family is our nature.

Perhaps the most profound examples and role models of love that I have experienced are the parents, spouses and children of people with chronic illnesses. These family members provide strong and informed family support. Whether it be intellectual or physical disorders – Alzheimer's, Parkinson's, multiple sclerosis, or schizophrenia, to name a few – day in and day out the family members prove that they are the true heroes in our community. They are largely unsung heroes. I work with supporting these family members with their chronically challenging and exhausting role. But what do they *do*? They love.

When we interact with others – loved ones, work ones, tricky ones – we are interacting with each individual's complexity and uniqueness. Each of these characters in our lives opens a doorway into another world – *their* world. Each of us has our unique life experiences and our stories of courage, joy and pleasure, as well as fear, sorrow and loss.

One problem is we don't realise that we are as much alike as we are. Men and women, different ethnicities, different religions, different cultures. We are much more alike than we are different. While we feel separate and different from others, we need to get it through our heads that we all share *the common experience of being human*. We all have our human needs; we all have our insecurities and our negative self-talk. If we could see that we are as alike as we are, we might feel safer and more comfortable joining together as a global family of humans. Corny as it is, it is true that we are all in this together, and we are currently doing a pretty bad job of looking after our home – our planet. Imagine if we extended our care globally, as we care for our own backyard and our own family.

What about when we get this human love thing wrong? Some of us feel a growing sense of alienation and disconnection from others. Our technology advancements border on miraculous, but many of us don't know our neighbours. Where are our advances in intimate connections with others? We might feel uncomfortable within ourselves; we may feel anxious or depressed, and this makes the bridge to connect with others feel absolutely too hard. How can we connect to others if we can't connect with ourselves? If we are feeling vulnerable, dealing with other people is too much.

Sometimes the problem is purely that we don't know *how* to connect to one another, and this makes us feel isolated from others. The only answer is to skill up and move towards the problem. Avoiding this fear hasn't worked, has it? In fact, our anxiety and bad habits of avoidance just get worse So, if the approach is not working, it's a good idea to change direction. Therapeutic support is a really good idea if this has become entrenched for you and you're finding it hard to move forward.

Another seismic problem is prejudice towards others, subtle or overt. Prejudice and ridiculing of differences is based on personal insecurity and fear. If I accept a person or a group that is different from me, then I am going to have to adjust my view of the world, or my (narrow) view of normal. I will feel less sure that my way of living is the right one, because this person or group is challenging my normal. If we were able to get a big shot in the arm of confidence and self-assuredness, then we would be able to respect and embrace other peoples' differences, because we would be more settled within ourselves; we wouldn't make it about *us*. Observing, learning and respecting others' differences would not even trigger us to think about ourselves. There would be no internal dialogue about it. We could sit back and enjoy the different textures and colours of the world and the people around us. We'd see that other peoples' worlds are *not* a threat to our 'normal'.

Do you have a big world or a small world? Do you see a narrow horizon or a wide horizon?

Have you noticed that people largely see what they expect to see? You could say that we get what we look for in life.

People who look for anger in others are usually fearful; people who look for betrayal in others are insecure or jealous; people who expect to be rejected or ostracised are insecure. People who look for reassurance from others are not able to reassure and soothe themselves. When we expect something from others as a general theme, we are often actually holding up a mirror. We are reflecting, or projecting, our insecurities and issues. Then we are imposing them on the poor sod across from us. Through our determined projection and looking, we do end up seeing what we expected to see. We have selective attention and we behave in a way that creates the expected reaction from others. Perhaps, unsurprisingly, they react to how we are behaving, and our expectation is fulfilled. We literally create our reality.

The good news is that the opposite works also. Positive projection. Setting ourselves up to receive positive behaviours from others sounds like a very good plan. If we look for the best in others, we often get it. If we smile and are welcoming in anticipation of a positive interaction, the other person can put down their defences and barriers and feel safe enough to show us their warm smiling side in turn.

A friend once remarked, 'The waitresses are so warm with you, but they're bitchy with me.' She didn't realise that this was directly because she carries herself with an elitist, snobby attitude. She does this to cover her anxieties and to try to feel in control. I personally live the warm approach, and I find the world is generally warm in response. The message is this: in order to have positive interactions with others, change yourself first.

We need to stop creating our own roadblocks and barriers when connecting with people. Initiate the contagious dance of positive warm social interaction. Doors and smiles open up for you. When you do experience connection with another, how do your mind and body feel?

Often clients present with their walls up, and we need to work towards making them feel safe enough to cut through these defences and be straight up with their inner worlds. I had one fellow who came in and spoke as if he was reading a police report. He wanted to sound official and commanding. He wanted to control the session and intimidate me. I called him on this at the end of the session, when we had cut through this façade. I told him that the real him was a much more enjoyable version. He replied, 'Yes, I can come across as strong and intimidating.' (He actually said these words!). I replied that he did not come across as intimidating at all, but rather that he came across as scared. This floored him. His façade was not working; it rarely does. I explained that if he was actually the confident person he was trying to come across as, that he would be able to relax and he would not need to impress or control the situation.

I often feel like there are two clients for every client. The initially wary client, who is either withdrawn or trying to put on a façade of some sort, and the real, authentic 'warts and all' client who comes out once they feel safe. The true person. It is rewarding to soften up their barricade till it melts away. My fantasy is that we could all see each other's heart, vulnerability and ego. Instead of reacting to each other's exterior, we would have love, compassion, and understanding. By not getting distracted and consumed by each other's façades, we could then feel calmer about ourselves, feel we are okay, more self-sufficient, and goofier. It would be like an ego truce throughout the world.

Humans are by nature complacent. We habituate to what we have and then we take it for granted, loving relationships included. We can bustle around with self-importance and career dramas, and not notice as our personal life is unravelling. We can end up with prosperity in the workforce but having lost our intimacy at home – and even intimacy with ourselves. Our determined work ethic gets out of balance with our home life, which affects our partnering and parenting obligations and domestic priorities. We can also become task-orientated in the home and not loved-one orientated: 'I don't have time to read to you, play with you, even hug you; I have washing to fold.' Pursuing accomplishments is great, but it should be done with a clear view of the impact and demand on personal relationships. This is about being incredibly sensible with allocating your life's energies.

We have five boys, and I have a private practice that has been bursting at the seams for sixteen years now.

Allocating life's energies would be my superhero power if I was to have one. I like the exercise of asking, 'If you have twenty-five parts to you, how many are allocated to yourself, your family and to your work?' Interesting question. How does this breakdown look right now? How do you want it to look, and how can you make those changes? What are your priorities?

There is no doubt: deep, nourishing relationships bring joy. We need to take the time to build our relationships with our partners, parents, siblings, children, friends and colleagues.

CHAPTER 2
KINDNESS & COMPASSION – RIPPLE EFFECT

One reason I decided to become a clinical psychologist is because I grew up with foster kids. Throughout my childhood, my mum fostered seventeen kids, mostly short- to mid-term. For three who were long term, my home was their childhood home. I saw many things; I witnessed many different mental health presentations. I have some interesting stories to share, but most of all, I saw first-hand the profound impact that receiving care, being listened to and being prioritised can have on a young person. I saw, right in front of my eyes, the healing and recovery that some level of stability could bring. From initial harsh shielding behaviour, they softened to show their beautiful tender side. But only when they started to feel safe.

It is a profound thing to realise the impact that you can have on another. I learnt or naturally had the capacity to witness another person in their vulnerability with compassion and without judgement. It is from this foundation that I grew a desire to understand, to become skilled and to offer my time and dedication to this healing profession. I also admire my mother enormously; she would have taken in more foster kids if she could. I believe lessons in kindness and compassion for others should be taught in schools, along with lessons on our 'humanness'.

> *If you want to be happy, practice compassion.*
> His Holiness the Dalai Lama

'Strong minds discuss ideas; average minds discuss events; weak minds discuss people.' I love this sentiment, which has been attributed in various forms to a range of wise people including Eleanor Roosevelt and Socrates. Even back in 390 BC, people were bitching about each other. And we all do it: daily gossip and criticism of colleagues, friends, family, celebrities ... anyone, really. Even if we don't buy the magazines, we read it in our news feed under the title 'entertainment'. We are ruthless; we cut down, we bitch, and we moan. Horrible human behaviour. Where is the compassion? Why do we presume to know anything about anyone or any situation? We have an armchair opinion. We are not part of the situation; how can we be an expert on other peoples' personal lives?

For breaches in ethical behaviour, political conflict across the world, environmental crises, absolutely have an opinion – but don't gossip. I like the response 'not my circus, not my monkeys'. It's none of my business. Again, how about compassion rather than judgement?

Here's a fun fact. The thoughts that you have about others shape your own experience. Every time you think negatively and judge others, you inflict pain on yourself, as that negative thought is felt by *you*, not them. *You* get the negative kick from that thought. The irony is rather beautiful and a bit wicked. You cannot be in a neutral to positive mind-state while you are busy being negative about others. It just doesn't work that way; you are experiencing a whisper to a wallop of negative thought and negative emotion. Jealousy, hostility, whining, complaining, bitching and moaning: who experiences those emotions? The person who is projecting them.

> *Be kind, for everyone you meet is fighting a hard battle.*
> – a quote attributed to Socrates, Philo, Plato and Ian Maclaren

Perhaps the best rule to live by is 'be kind'. We need kindness in the world, so treat people with kindness. A close cousin to kindness is compassion. Compassion involves understanding and genuine comprehension of the other person's position, and feeling empathy and a desire for their suffering to resolve. It means being able to understand the sorrows and the pains of the other person.

Compassion for our loved ones or even strangers is not too difficult if we prioritise it, put our mind to it and extend ourselves into their worlds. What is challenging is compassion for those who have harmed us. Compassion is the opposite of hate; it is the opposite of ugly, vengeful thoughts. I am not suggesting that you should dismiss harm that someone has done to you, or that you should not advocate for or protect yourself – absolutely not. But you can, while understanding of the wrongness of their behaviour, also have compassion for the mess that they are digging themselves into. If their behaviour is ugly to others, they are left with their own ugly selves. This understanding and compassion for them takes away the negative hot emotions that you are experiencing. You are really doing yourself an enormous favour. The hate that you feel is toxic to *you*, not to them. If you can manifest compassion for them then you can have a release, a distancing from your negative emotions.

And what about the ripple effect of kindness? The ripple effect goes out to others through a lifting of their experience, and they in turn will be in a better place within themselves, which will then affect their behaviour towards others. The kindness ripple effect also radiates throughout your emotional experience. When we behave with love towards others, we literally draw love back to us and our experience is brightened. What you give out, you experience yourself. You mirror and receive the warmth of kindness.

CHAPTER 3
WHAT IS LOVE?

What is love? We can list off many positive behaviours and feelings – deep affection, trust, mutual respect, companionship – when we define love. Unconsciously, however, we actually have a different understanding of love. The question is not actually, 'What is love?' The question is, 'What is your reference point of love?' or 'In your experience of love, what has been familiar to you?'

The concept of love actually comes through in our behaviour, and it often is not a pretty picture. What we behaviourally seek out can be very different to our ideal of love. We have formed a template in our subconscious that outlines what we have experienced, what we are familiar with, and what we are strangely comfortable with. So what is *your* reference point for love? What is your template? What is your normal?

We seek out other relationships to replicate what has been our previous experiences of love. If you have had healthy relationships growing up, or with previous partners, then your reference point for love is likely to be healthy. If you then come across someone who mistreats you, this will clash with your experience of love, your sense of normal, and you are most likely not going to put up with this. You will exit the relationship. If you have had previous experiences of neglect or abuse, then sadly this is your reference point, this is your normal. If we've been neglected, we look for neglect in our next partner. If we have been abused, criticised or put down, we are in danger of looking for this in our future partner. The list goes on.

Consciously, we can't stand these negative traits; we complain about them and we gnash our teeth about them, but here is the thing: behaviourally we keep being drawn to them. In its worst form, this is the essence of the domestic violence cycle and the reason it continues to recur despite the lack of rational logic. Remember the saying, 'We marry our father'? It's scary how much truth is in this. You protest, 'This is rubbish; I don't want to believe this.' Understandable. But this is how it works; in this situation, the template for receiving healthy love is missing.

When you have an unhealthy reference point for love, even if you find yourself in a relationship that you can consciously see is unhealthy and distressing, it will feel *familiar*. You have set your bar low. You are likely to accept it, play down the problems and not be aware enough of the danger clues. Sadly, you are likely to stay.

It gets worse; if you have a history of experiencing neglect or abuse, you are in danger of shutting down potentially healthy relationships because they make you feel uncomfortable. It feels weird and foreign to be treated well. It is not your normal; you don't know what to do with that behaviour, or feel that you don't deserve it. You might feel your partner is better than you, and that they might eventually realise that you're not good enough. You might become scared that they will leave you. You might even try to simplify this with 'They're too nice', or 'I'm used to the bad boys'.

We need to have conscious awareness of what we are doing and consider what is our background, our fears, our patterns. What do you notice? Through conscious awareness we need to decide to change our patterns and create healthy new experiences of normal, to be brave enough to get unfamiliar and uncomfortable as we grow and heal. This means putting ourselves in healthy situations and learning to receive healthy care and love from our important others – partners and friends.

If we have had a negative experience of love and we come across a healthy partner, we might literally squirm receiving their consideration. We don't know what to do, think, or how to react when they care about our opinion. We do not think we deserve their standard of behaviour and we can be riddled with dread that they are not really going to want us long term – that they are too 'good' for us. With a neglectful or abusive partner, we at least feel secure that they are not too good for us. Our self-worth has been so damaged by our previous, dysfunctional relationships that we do not have the self-love template to receive healthy love.

What patterns do you have that repeat in your life? Personally, I had an emotionally neglectful father who never really knew me, and I grew up with a whole lot of emotional volatility. Despite my stable and loving mother, I felt like I grew up on the edge of a volcano, waiting for it to explode, and developed much skill in ducking the lava when it did. So what did I look for in my early relationships? Neglect. And what did I tolerate? Emotional volatility. Even when a partner had the capacity to be loving and willing, I could not take or ask for my share. I did not know how to have a voice, as I had survived my childhood by being invisible. I was the opposite of a demanding child, so as an adult I found it hard to assert my needs in a healthy way.

On the very positive side, I learnt self-love and I have always been very confident and positive within myself and towards others. I have always had a bouncy, optimistic and ambitious approach to life. This was clearly shaped by my mother's unwavering capacity to value, support and celebrate my strengths. The confidence she had in me became self-assuredness within myself. I had a resoundingly positive experience of love from my mother, which was not only my life raft and my launching pad, but also a positive template for how to give and receive love.

I therefore had both healthy and unhealthy templates for love, which influenced me in different ways at different times. This is a brief analysis of my historical love template and the impact on my adult relationships. It would be a profound investment and gift to yourself to analyse *your* love templates and your adult relationship patterns. Study yourself, get clear within yourself, write it down. You cannot get healthy with your love templates if you are not an expert on them.

If you're stuck in an unhealthy pattern, you can and definitely need to break the cycle. This is the good news. Learn your patterns. What role do you keep playing in your relationships? *You* are the common denominator. Once you know this pattern, you can match it up with your conscious expectations for love, for a healthy relationship, for a healthy daily partnership. And you can choose to get uncomfortable with being treated well, with having someone communicate respectfully and lovingly. You can learn to be a priority and to have a voice. If, intellectually, you *know* what is happening is healthy, and if you feel uncomfortable receiving this love, then you are on track. Now you just have to sit in this discomfort, understanding what is happening. You are growing; you are healing. Just sit with it until over time it becomes your new normal; then you will have built the internal template to receive the loving behaviours.

I recall when *I* finally figured it out. I was excruciatingly uncomfortable with my beautiful Jon when he would care to understand me. He was gentle and mindful towards me and made me feel I had a voice; I was a priority. What I gave in relationships, I was finally receiving back.

Crudely speaking, there are givers and takers in the world. Takers want givers, and givers want givers. The key is to spot the takers. This is a tough job as they know that they are not desirable as takers, so they masquerade as givers until they feel secure in the relationship; then they unzip the costume and there is the wolf in sheep's clothing. They want to receive love, not give love. And if we have an unhealthy history with our experience of love, we are all too ready to subconsciously tolerate the wolf's version of love when he lets his superficial shield down.

What about the extent of our love? We clearly have deep and strong love when, day in, day out, we place the importance of our loved one's desires and needs on the level of our own. This can be tricky as it competes with the necessity to also have a healthy care for our own needs. I would ask: would you risk your life for theirs? If we would not contemplate this, how can we say that we love them?

There is also the issue of **unconditional love** and **conditional love** Simply speaking, I would argue that *we only really have unconditional love for our children.* Sounds harsh, but in a healthy way we need to have some level of boundaries or conditions for our relationships with our partners, friends, even parents and siblings. Here's the test: sorry to provoke, but if you found out your loved one had done some heinous crime, such as rape or paedophilia, would you visit them in jail? Would you keep them in your life? Would you love them still, with no conditions? If your partner did these things, it would be wise to reconsider your relationship so, no, you don't have unconditional love for your partner. You need to have healthy conditions and boundaries. There are deal-breaking behaviours in our relationships. But if your *child* had committed those crimes, I would argue that you would probably find a way through – that you would not at all condone their behaviour, but with boundaries, you would find a way to stay involved with them. Hence, true unconditional love.

Perhaps the most important thing in life is to learn to love and be loved. Now we know that we cannot just work with our subconscious version of what this looks like. We have to check that our version of love, our 'normal' and 'familiar' love, is actually good for us. Many of us fear love, believing that we don't deserve it. We fear it will open us up to being vulnerable, so we become our own roadblock to living fully. That is what this book is trying to hammer home: if it's broken, fix it, and here's some direction regarding how.

It is worth our while to learn to love well. There are profound returns on that investment. I once heard somewhere 'Love is the only rational act'. I agree. Do you?

CHAPTER 4
PARTNER WELL

Love is absolutely vital for a human life. When you learn to love, and let yourself be loved, you feel held and awakened at the same time, as if you're in a warm shelter from which you can go out into the world. We *want* to love and to be loved. We want to feel understood, cherished, accepted and celebrated for who we are. As my dear friend June once said to me, 'It's biology'. We are designed to 'pair bond', like so many other species. I know people whose 'pair bond' is their dearest friend, not actually a partner. They are inseparable and spend their days together – two peas in a pod. Nothing sexual, just deep love and rich and safe companionship. However it works for you is fine; whatever the gender, two souls are connected and nourished by each other. That is the bottom line.

The research is clear that marriage is a protective factor for our physical health and our happiness state. Research looks at 'marriage' for ease of definition for data collection, but this really applies to long-term committed relationships. I will refer to 'marriage', but what I am really referring to is long-term defacto relationships, in all gender combinations. Of course, the enormous amount of research on the positive effects of marriage would be more meaningful if it first tested for healthy versus unhealthy marriages. As we know there are plenty of toxic marriages that persist because of convention, lack of choice and interpersonal fears. But nevertheless, the over-arching outcome of the research is that marriage is good for us.

Our partner ought to be the person who treats us the best. The person who we are most emotionally safe with. They are in our corner. They look after us as we look after them. Your relationship with your person is a dance in which you can spin around at great speed because you have each other. Have high standards. If you are going to be a quality partner and an asset to the person you're with, then it is very important that your expectations are that your partner will enrich your life. You deserve a partner who makes you feel safe so you can be exactly who you are and speak your truth. Someone who never intimidates or threatens you and who communicates openly about everything, from the good things to the things that drive you nuts. Your partner needs to embrace exactly who you are so that you flourish daily. Don't settle for a partner who offers you anything else.

If you were going for a one-year road trip, you would know that your travelling companion would make or break the experience. How carefully would you choose your travelling companion – asking yourself whether you are compatible, and how you complement and enrich each other? Wondering what it will be like to be with them on their 'off' days, in the hard times? How essential would it be for you to be an expert on them? This is a great example of how important it is to partner well – but extend the timeframe and the ramifications to *life*. One of the most important decisions you will ever make is who you bring into your life as your partner. And this is tough. We have made advances in almost all fields, but we have not gained much insight into why we choose the people we do.

As children we seek the unconditional approval of our parents, and emotional security is our ultimate goal. We continue to want this security in our partner. This is our desire to be accepted just as we are. What we are looking for is someone who can be a lifelong companion, who can affirm our worth, who shall soften the blows of aging through mutual care and love. The happiness of finding love is the greatest thing in all of the world. This is **pair bonding**: a close, nurturing relationship, where we can be intimately understood and seen. When we feel understood, we feel like we are home. Being understood creates our sense of belonging; it lets us feel free to be ourself.

Sadly, many are sceptical that this kind of secure pair bonding is possible. It seems out of their reach and they may not believe that healthy people are out there or that they are worthy of a healthy person. This disillusionment only creates another barrier. We present with our brick walls, our shields, our negativity, and we receive a cautious defensive response from others in turn (which we interpret as rejection). We need to have the courage to be totally vulnerable with our partner. This is risky. Most of us have experienced or will experience the devastation of discovering we were mistaken in our trust in another. These wounds understandably lead to cynicism. We're not going to open ourselves up to these emotional risks if we don't believe the goal of a secure, healthy relationship is possible.

Think about it, though: if you can be healthy in *your* half of the relationship, why should you not presume that there are plenty of people out there who can match you and love you right back? And if you don't feel as if you are able to hold up your end of the bargain, then get started on your 'hot issues'. We all need to be ambitious in having healthy, thriving relationships. A healthy love relationship shapes your life and your every day.

To partner well we need to be prepared to be generous of heart and invest our time and energy. To partner well we also need to not be in a hurry to find someone. If we are rushing in because we are filling a hole, a desire to feel loved and secure, we are likely not to be as selective as we need to be. We also need to take the time to know who we are first, and to work out what we want in a partner. It is so important to pace yourself because you want the right one, not just the next one.

You could argue that our culture is becoming a bit commitment phobic in the dating game and, as a result, we discard each other too freely. Those being discarded act tough because they don't want to expose their vulnerability, but when you like someone, you are looking for affirmation that they like you back, and so this cavalier approach can be damaging. Our hearts and self-esteem are on the line when we as a society get too casual about dating or pre-dating.

Many take this concept of commitment at the early stages of dating way too seriously. If you are special to each other and if your exploring of each other is exclusive, with no other players involved, then just face it: you are dating. This means valuing each other enough to take the time to learn, explore and enjoy each other. This is being a girlfriend or boyfriend, but without making a big commitment. You are just seeing what happens. With time and connection in your lives this dating situation might evolve into a romantic partnership.

Of course, when we are afraid to refer to the person that we are dating as our 'girlfriend' or 'boyfriend', they can feel insecure, discouraged and hurt. There is a tendency in our culture to panic about putting words to this dating stage. It is not actually that we need to label anything, but the act of rejecting the term girlfriend/boyfriend can make the individual feel discarded. They are in this stage of being exclusive and exploring each other. During this stage of becoming more open with each other, there is a danger in not using the appropriate language to show that you value each other. It can leave you feeling vulnerable and exposed.

It needn't be this way because dating is not a heavy commitment. Having a 'girlfriend' or 'boyfriend' is not a heavy commitment. If the relationship doesn't have legs and longevity, it ends; you're not locked in. So why do people freak out and deny that they are special to each other? This is damaging. It can make us can feel invisible. And of course, feeling denied in our specialness to each other is actually going to get in the way of the relationship's growth. Maybe we need to go back to old-school language and simply 'date'. Just relax, take it slow, enjoy each other, but don't deny each other's specialness.

Another big barrier to finding 'our person' is a fear of the 'rejection dance' on our first meeting. What if we don't like them, or they don't like us? Well here is the thing. It's quite simple: you're not in control. You could meet a really great person, but you may not have chemistry; you may not be drawn to them. Why do we fall in love with one person and not another? **Pheromones** play an interesting role here. Pheromones are similar to hormones, but they work outside the body and induce a sexual response in others. They are the sexual scent of attraction.

Research indicates that our pheromones are clever in helping us make stronger, healthier children in that we usually smell best to a person whose genetically based immunity to disease differs the most from our own. This usually leads to a better genetic pool for our offspring. So you might be a real catch but the person you are meeting might just not feel the chemistry for you. This is okay.

Dating is not a test to determine who is up there with the dating points; it really is influenced by our primal pheromone attraction, which we do not control.

Often we find ourselves attracted to someone we know is bad for us, and we don't feel attraction for someone who we know ticks all the boxes. It's roll the dice; it's not even intelligent. So if we can see 'rejection' as not personal, then we won't see it as being a reflection of whether we are okay or not. And if *you* are not attracted to someone, then the trick is to communicate this directly and with care: 'I really can see you are a great person and I've enjoyed our time, but I just don't feel any chemistry.' And be prepared to have this said to you in turn.

And for goodness' sake, you cannot gauge your feelings for a person until you are face-to-face in real time. Social media, phone calls or video calls do not cut it. Online there is no ability to test your chemistry; you have to be in physical contact for this. On these media you can park a conversation for when it suits you; you do not need to spend time together during good times and bad. You also do not have access to the majority of interpersonal information, which includes essential non-verbal communication such as facial cues, body language, voice tone and timing.

One version of dating tragedy is of course unrequited interest in another. They like you but you don't feel it, or you like them, but they don't feel it. Ouch! But it happens; it is part of the game. You cannot control these things.

We keep flipping the coin until we both land 'heads up', and we both feel the chemistry and desire to advance things and get to know each other better. Hang in there; it's a numbers game. The negative/negative, the positive/negative, the negative/positive ... and then – hooray! – we get a positive/positive. You've got to be in it to finally get a good outcome. This is not personal; it's just that you have to wait until there is a matching of pheromones and minds.

Time to be brave. Feel the fear and do it anyway.

CHAPTER 5
HONEYMOON PHASE: BECOME AN EXPERT ON THEIR 'UGLY'

So we have worked out what love is. It is not one universal concept; in reality it is our old patterns – our past experiences – wanting to repeat and repeat into our future. It is our job to know our dodgy love programming and update it, and learn to receive and require a healthy version of love. Let's flesh it out more and look at the launching part of the relationship.

In each stage in the process of deciding if a partner is 'the one', we face different obstacles. Let's have a look:

1. Our brains go into a less-than-rational phase, the 'honeymoon' phase;
2. Often we can delude ourselves and impose on our partner what we want them to be; and
3. We become an expert on them – not just their shiny self, but their ugly side as well.

We need to learn how to steer ourselves through this crazy time.

HONEYMOON BRAIN

Dating involves joint exploration. We are inquiring into the motives and patterns of our potential partner's thoughts and behaviours. We are wanting to understand them, their past influences and their future intentions, values and priorities. So are we going to do this interviewing process with a rational and calm brain? No! We are doing this crucial interview process with our 'honeymoon phase' brain. The honeymoon phase is the magical time when our partner is fairly perfect in our eyes and we are very much in love. We feel passionate, intense feelings of attraction and ecstasy, as well as an idealisation of our partner. Amongst other changes in our brain chemistry, our brains are flushed with **dopamine**, a chemical messenger associated with reward and motivation.

Our concept of romantic love and our attempts to find a partner are coloured by the honeymoon phase that is milked in romantic movies. We can even start thinking that this delirious, slightly delusional phase is actually what a relationship looks like. Then when some reality seeps back into our lives we can think that there is a problem. We would much rather stay in our romantic paradise mindset. When we are besotted, we are overly generous. It's hard to bring this intoxicated, loving, delirious state back to analytical and rational thought – to be able to look and see the clues that will show us the full picture of the person we are falling in love with. Please know that this blind love stage is real. It's not you personally, it is you being a messy human. It's hard – near impossible – to navigate once you are struck. None of us are immune.

This honeymoon phase, 'falling in love', can be a mindless fantasy that draws us in and has us spinning. The sheer lack of rational brainpower during this phase sets us up for disappointment. When the honeymoon phase passes, we crash back to reality with the true person that we have signed up for. They may be a gem; they may have a beautiful heart and be a wonderful and caring companion and we may have chosen well. But they also may not be a good choice, or they may be a lovely person but not compatible for your life journey. When our relationship has started with this sudden, powerful or seemingly spiritual appeal, this sudden wave of feeling has us skip the gentle stage of building a friendship that can provide a deep, profound and exciting bond. Friendship takes time, clear learning and communication, and a rational brain to build.

The key is to learn to *watch ourselves* go down the rabbit hole of the honeymoon phase. Have a sense of humour with peculiar behaviour that lacks sound reasoning. It is pretty crazy that when we have the experience of 'falling in love' we behave as if that is all we need to start a relationship. We don't apply any sound logic to forming this attachment; we base it on our mysterious chemistry and our physical attraction.

By contrast, if we break up, we explain to ourselves and others the sound reasoning behind our decision. The key is to have the formula of feeling the chemistry, but at the same time slow down and make sure this person is a healthy and sound choice for us. To do this we need to steer our crazy honeymoon brain chemistry; we need to stay sensible. We need to decide whether to let the feelings grow. If they seem like healthy partner material, let the feelings grow. If they are looking like a more negative cluster of thinking and behaviour, then don't let the feelings grow – run away!

THREE IN THE BED

If you are in a relationship and you meet a third party with whom you feel this chemistry hit, you need to be extremely careful, wise and sensible. You need to take responsibility not to engage with this person. Either you're in an exclusive relationship and this third person will rock its foundation or, if you're in a relationship that's floundering, you need to sort that out first, independent of this third person. Take responsibility for the direction that this will go and don't allow time with this new love interest. Don't be naïve; if you fuel this relationship, then these feeling will grow. Affairs do not just happen. They do not sneak up on us; we fuel the brain chemistry to allow them to grow.

We are responsible. Meanwhile, if you want to maintain your committed relationship, work on it – because something is very wrong if you are looking elsewhere.

There will be plenty of people in our future who we will feel an attraction to, who will activate our pheromones. This is inevitable; this is human nature. The key is whether we are looking around and whether we allow ourselves to be open to this pathway. If your committed relationship is ending, clean up that chapter first in a healthy way before opening up another new relationship chapter. Otherwise you will risk not doing justice to either relationship.

Seeking out novelty in partners is really about seeking reassurance. As we age and we realise that death is not a thing that just happens to other people, we might flirt with others in order to feed our conceit that we are still attractive. We want others to seek us out and to tell us that we are desirable. Sex with someone new can give us this brief jolt of reassurance. However, this reassurance quickly evaporates.

WISHFUL PROJECTION

One of our human tragedies is the tendency to bundle up our personal strengths, our spark, all the positive and wonderful things in our lives, and then project them onto the person that we are dating. Perhaps most human behaviour is driven by intentions that are outside of our conscious awareness. We do not like to concede this. We think of ourselves as rational people. We think we can explain our behaviour. We don't like to think that a lot of our habitual behaviour is driven by our past experiences, our desires and our needs.

People joke about psychologists wanting to know about our childhoods. There is a very good reason for this: it is these early experiences that shape us, and many of the lessons that we have taken on are below our consciousness. A perfect example of this subconscious dance is that our actions in choosing a partner are much more a reflection of ourselves than the other person we are supposedly choosing. During the honeymoon phase, we project our own positives onto our potential partner, all without our conscious awareness. We do this strange thing where we cannot necessarily see these strengths in ourselves, but we decide we see them in the other person because *it is what we want in our other. We are projecting our value system on to them.* Instead of realising that *we* are the source of the wonder in our lives, we put our prospective partner on a pedestal.

Loving someone is very different from falling in love. When we fall in love, our brain chemistry goes haywire and we make the other person angelic in our eyes. Perhaps this is the cave dweller in us; we are designed to become besotted and procreate with our new mate. The primary goal is having babies, not necessarily looking for a solid lifelong cave companion. Or perhaps it is to avoid being led by our fears and therefore being negative and sceptical. Perhaps without the honeymoon phase we would remain behind our barriers and not partner up? When someone is about to tell you that they have met someone and they are besotted, you can literally read it on their face and in their eyes before they say anything. It is amazing. I get to test this theory regularly at work and I don't think I have ever got it wrong. You don't need to be a psychologist to see that they are gushing.

We idolise during the honeymoon phase. No one can live up to this idolisation. No one is truly the angel we see, and eventually this projection wears thin. Some people fail to learn about themselves and their patterns here, and when the initial flames of passion cool, they rush off to fall in love with someone else, only to have the same pattern repeat again and again. They are the serial honeymooner. They do not step back and realise that they are in a meaningless cycle, always getting on the same Ferris wheel.

KNOW THEIR 'UGLY'

Much of the pain and heartache that we experience in life comes from our failure to recognise the personality characteristics that make someone an unhealthy choice for a committed relationship. This of course means that these relationships are difficult and often not sustainable.

Finding someone who shares your value system and has healthy personality traits is crucial. If you don't have a common set of values in life, then as a couple, you are in hot water. Your values need to be aligned. Negative traits tend to cluster, and positive traits tend to cluster. What this means is that when you find someone with a host of negative traits, they tend to have a whole lot more negative traits that you just haven't discovered yet. The same goes for someone with a pattern of positive traits. Keep getting to know them and you'll usually find a treasure trove of more positive strengths to enjoy. This positive and negative cluster pattern is not always the case, but it is a good rule of thumb.

The key is to spot these traits in a potential partner, which is really tricky because when someone has these negative traits, they often know the traits are not attractive or desirable. They may therefore work very hard to present well and to cover up their true selves. Are they a sheep, or a wolf in sheep's clothing? The negative cluster traits are self-centredness, impulsivity, lack of insight and poor anger regulation. The positive cluster traits are kindness, insight, empathy, the ability to laugh at oneself, communicate and not need to win, and a capacity for generous love, ownership of one's limitations, and apology.

> Look at their ego, their vulnerability and their core, not at their façade.

In working out whether our potential partner is generally from the positive cluster or the negative cluster, we need to pay attention not to what they promise but to how they behave. The most reliable predictor of future behaviour is past behaviour. It is so essential to focus on behaviour; it is the only communication that can be truly trusted. When there is a discrepancy between what they say and do, or between their good behaviour and their behaviour when they are stressed or not on show, we sometimes choose to ignore incongruent behaviours. They clash with the idealisation going on in our honeymoon brain.

Do you know who they really are?

Let's talk about warning signs that we have not chosen a great partner:

1. They have poor insight, are unwilling to take responsibility and they are not comfortable saying 'I'm sorry'. They are unable to laugh at themselves, and they are defensive and not open to learning about themselves.

2. They are overly concerned with public image and their behaviour behind closed doors is in marked contrast to what they show the world. Away from public eyes their own value system regarding how they treat others is not healthy. Do you know who they really are?

3. They focus on *their* needs, not yours, and they prefer to take rather than give. When they give, it somehow also becomes about them.

4. Rather than focusing on calmly building and nurturing your world and your confidence, they tend to create drama and instability. They cut down, rather than build up.

UNDERBELLY

In public and when we are trying to impress and attract a partner, we are presenting our *social face* or our *ideal self*. We are on our best behaviour, mindful of the other person's impression of us. We are usually keeping our vulnerabilities private and following social convention – doing and being what is expected of us in the world. But under the surface of how we are in public and how we are when we want to impress our new partner, is our other self: our self on a bad day. You can think of it as our *underbelly*, our *hidden, private self*, our *true self*. If the person is a bit of a bad egg, they may actively hide their true self and replace it with a fake 'good behaviour' version.

For most people, their underbelly, or true self, is not a big leap from their social self. It is just a more vulnerable, quieter version. They can get grumpy, be less patient and stuff up, but their underbelly is still a tolerable picture. Their underbelly is not a deal breaker. We can even find it endearing as we know their value system is well intenced and harmless.

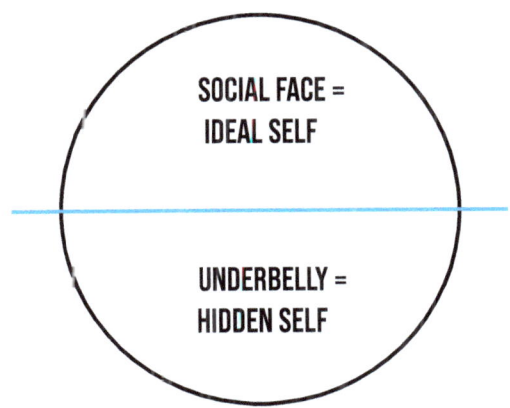

By contrast, the people who are more like wolves in sheeps' clothing know that if you saw their true selves from the outset you would walk the other way. They hide their underbelly because it has negative cluster traits like those listed above. They actively hide their true selves until you are in a secure and committed relationship and they feel that you are not as free to leave them. They then relax and show their ugly selves, and they impose these ugly behaviours upon you. They launch their anger at you, impose their needs selfishly, manipulate and undermine you. Often they'll show their underbelly after you have got married, you have bought a house together or you have had a child together. If you are luckier, they will foolishly expose their true ugly selves to you before you are in too deep – and, hopefully, you'll run!

But there is good news. There will be leaks in their social mask; there will be clues to their true underbelly self. The key is to be alert to them and, when they appear, do not generously dismiss them as the rarity. Ask the question, 'What sort of value system would allow them to behave this way?'

It is extremely wise to test the relationship with stress before you become committed. If you have no kids in the picture, then living together with low commitment (not shared finances) is a great way to see each other's true selves. But just remember: you are roommates testing each other out. You are not locked in. Don't jump in and share bank accounts and give away your furniture. Stay capable of your independence until this thorough interview process in complete. How are they as a team player? How are they with finances; do they take or give? How are they when in conflict with you and others? How are they when they are tired and stressed, and things are not going their way? Travelling to tricky destinations where tiredness, challenges and stress will occur is a brilliant idea.

Listen to loved ones if they are sound reasoners and they have concerns. They may be more objective than you. Keep your eyes open. You must truly be an expert about your potential partner. You must know their underbelly before you decide that they are your life partner. I am being super, super clear here!

CHAPTER 6
RELATIONSHIP EVOLVING ... STAGES

Falling in love is very different to staying in love. They are very different worlds. They are the *acceleration* of the relationship and then the *journey* of the relationship.

There are so many pathways to our relationship stories. Some people establish relationships early in life and the relationship grows with them. Others find that their expectations of life and who they grow to be cause the relationship to fall apart. Their early romantic relationship ends. There are those who stay single seemingly forever and do or do not find their life partner, and there are those who have several significant relationships, each taking up a formative chapter of their lives. What is essential is that we do not try to assume a template for relationship patterns in life. We can't presume we will get it right the first time. The picture doesn't need to be neat in life. What matters is learning and strengthening through life and growing through life experience, whether this be in one long-term relationship or several significant relationships. The last thing we need to do is try to fit a mould set by society.

The meaning of life is to love and be loved.

What we do know about relationships is that we move from the honeymoon phase to a more stable, building phase. We might see this as a dampening of the relationship, when in fact it is a coming out of the delicious honeymoon fog. Our job is to follow this honeymoon phase with an exciting and rewarding building and creating stage. This is where we are moving forward in life together in a mutually inspiring way. This is up to us. When we mindfully nurture and create healthy relationships, there is inexplicable joy and growth to be experienced. To love and be loved: this is perhaps what it is all about. Family life is ultimately our safe launch pad to developing a rich sense of ourselves, and our secure base from which we can then tackle the world.

Never allow disrespect or presumption to grow.

I LOVE YOU

We love to hear the reassuring and powerful message of 'I love you'. When in the context of a healthy relationship, these words affirm our experience in the relationship. When 'I love you' is said in isolation and there is not loving behaviour, these words are confusing and entrapping.

Perhaps these words are a promise of things that will change, and if so, they convey a confused hope for the receiver.

When there is a disconnect between what we say and what we do, we are being a hypocrite. It is important that we pay attention to *actions* here, not words. *Talk is cheap.* Unfortunately, we routinely get sucked in by empty words because they appeal to our blind hope for improvement and our sometimes futile hope that our needs will be met. We prescribe and impose our hopes for the future, so we are often ready and willing to be seduced by reassuring words even when they are in contrast to unloving actions. The reassuring words provide a comforting illusion that is hard to let go of. We want our partner to love us, and we want to believe their words and justify or dismiss their actions.

So how do we *show* love? How do we love through our actions? What actions count the most? We show love by listening to each other, knowing each other, considering each other, and through all the small, mundane things that we do for each other that show we matter to each other. Some people value thoughtful and generous gestures; some gifts; some quality time together; some mindful affection; some verbal connectedness. Love requires talking openly, deep respect for each other, and the clear commitment to work towards compromise. These are of course shown through our actions. We care about our partner prioritising us, especially with the quality and amount of time they want to spend with us. When actions match words, we can feel and trust that we are loved.

STAY YOUR OWN IDENTITY

You are two canoes gliding together on the journey of life. You are not in one canoe where you have to *become* each other and assimilate into the same person. You do not have the right to control the other person (it's their canoe!). It is often your differences and your uniqueness that first attracted you to each other. You can draw on your differences to collaborate and have a larger toolbelt in approaching your lives together. It is vital to stay within and honour your own identity.

We are always growing and continuing to refine our own self. You need enough space and enough voice in your relationship so that your personal growth continues, and you do not lose yourself. While we do need to be extremely mindful of each other in our choices, it is important that we don't place barriers or limits on each other – that we don't place each other in a prison.

Controlling behaviour can be due to a desire for or illusion of creating security. If you do feel that you have lost your own identity or you feel that you have not developed as an individual, this does not mean that you have to leave the relationship. Not at all. Provided your partner is not controlling or restricting you, it just means taking a small step sideways and creating time and space to reconnect with yourself – your current and expanding self. This is a time for reconnection within yourself while having the support of your relationship. What are your priorities, your preferences, your ambitions, your lifestyle choices? Take the time, work it through; this is not a sprint. We are going for an ongoing, quality outcome here.

I know many couples who have found their priorities and their voice, and they are light years away from each other, but they work out how to meet each other's needs. In one couple I know, she likes to take an overseas trip with a friend every two years, while he is an absolute homebody. He is truly content in his home life, feeding the menagerie of animals that are his 'children'. Another couple has found that the husband wants to travel for three months at a time on a shoestring, but his wife does not. She is content to be home doing her own thing; she feels no stress as he is financially so frugal, and he enjoys this financial challenge and is content in having his needs met. They are okay with this time apart because it is so important to him and she enjoys her own company, and on other occasions they travel together in a way that suits her better. These couples do not impose their needs on each other. They find a way to make the most of their differences and work out how to meet both of their needs. Being truly happy for each other in the pursuit of their priorities is so important. This generates a relaxed enthusiasm for each other, which allows for a positive experience. There is no resentment or belief that their partner ought to be like them.

There is no doubt: in our healthy relationships we need to celebrate our differences. Celebrate that the other person does not need to be a clone of us. How boring if we were all the same, cardboard cut-outs of each other. A lovely conversation you might have is to list ways that you have a different approach to things and different opinions. We need to celebrate this difference, and of course not see the other person as wrong. For example, I love horse riding; I grew up horse riding and it is a highlight for me. My beautiful Jon does not, and while of course I think he is missing out, I respect his opinion. And of course he has plenty of interests that I don't share. On the flipside, we both love scuba diving (I am a tourist and he is a professional free diver and scuba diver; we are a scuba family). Travel, quality food, long walks, and talking through our next project are also interests we share. It's wonderful to share passions and it's equally important to celebrate our differences.

NO TRAPPING

Conservative pressure sometimes makes us stay in dysfunctional relationships and mask our voice and our needs. It is extraordinary how many people have presented to me with the initial brag of 'We've been together for fifteen years, twenty-five years, thirty-five years, forty-five.' This is a practised opening line. Okay, no problem. But my opinion is paused until I hear about the *quality* of the lives that they share and bring to each other.

I often then hear that they are living in misery together. Their relationship is the number one cause of their daily anguish. Their needs are neglected and there is often an abusive dynamic. Yet they brag about their years together.

I have even had clients whose lives have become liberated and they have launched forward when their partners have passed away. This is a very confronting and sad realisation. Many have told me how lonely they feel in their marriage. I have also interestingly had waves of client families in which the parents are clearly in a dysfunctional relationship, but they state that they are 'staying together for the kids'. Meanwhile the kids are literally telling me, 'I wish Mum and Dad would get it together and separate; it's so unhealthy.' Either the parents are off track about what is best for their kids and believe that they are creating a healthier home by staying in a dysfunctional relationship, or they are hiding behind the 'doing it for the kids' mantra as an excuse to avoid the big adjustment of separation. It is quality of relationship that counts, not quantity of years together. These individuals are blindly swallowing society's values of staying together at all costs. To them, this is the picture of success, to the outside world at least.

It was only a few decades ago that partners were forced to stay together due to strangling societal pressures and lack of financial support. Divorce was rare, though this didn't mean that relationships were more positive. Lack of choice to leave would have played an enormous role in deciding to stay together. Also, with the traditional roles and a lack of support resources, couples were more dependent on each other. The husbands needed someone to cook, care for the children and look after the house. There was no childcare and men were often not very domestic in their gender role. Wives were dependent on their husbands for income. There was simply a need for each other. Sadly, this often led to partners taking advantage and abusing this mutual dependence.

We lament the increasing divorce rate but, while marriage and divorce should not be undertaken lightly, our current divorce rate is actually a reflection of choice and having resources of support. In my clinical experience, our divorce rate is largely a reflection of us not being trapped due to circumstance.

STAY FRESH; THERE'S NO ROOM FOR STALENESS

When we are in the throes of the honeymoon phase, we are busy getting to know each other. When we then progress to the building stage of the relationship it is time to launch into a whole new sphere of doing and expanding. This is important because we have become increasingly familiar with each other at this stage and we need to ward off the dangers of finding each other predictable and falling into a boring routine. We do not want the relationship to be based on mutual convenience. The complete novelty of each other has passed. While we do always continue to learn and discover new things about each other, our focus needs to be on continued mutual enjoyment and new areas of shared growth and passion. We need to continue to find new challenges and areas to refine, learn from and experiment with.

This of course is about experiencing the **state of flow** in our relationship, which means learning new meaningful things and having new meaningful experiences together that challenge us. This is about sometimes varying our daily routines. It involves expanding to continued new topics of conversation, expanding our friendship circles, and doing new things and going to new places. We are complex creatures. We provide each other with a wealth of variety, just in continuing to get to know each other in increasing depth. We need to pay attention to this complexity in each other and explore and celebrate it.

If you decide that you are healthy and compatible enough to be life partners then your adventures together create a wealth of variety. You create a home, a lifestyle, raise a family perhaps, expand your work horizons, get involved in the community, travel, grow hobbies, passions and aspirations for your medium and distant future. Keep fuelling these involvements together, using your relationship as the springboard from which to bounce off into your daily experiences and aspirations. There is no room for mundane monotony in life.

It's great to have a date with your partner at least once per month. My pick is actually once per week. During this date night, it is important that both of you consciously work to be partners, not parents. Try to leave the kid talk or household talk for another time. I know couples who have fun with 'first date conversation starters' that you can download. This fun prompting gets them to think outside of themselves. This is precious time to communicate, understand and relate to each other on an adult, deep but playful level.

PRACTISE, PRIORITISE, MAKE EFFORT, PAY ATTENTION

If you don't water a plant it will die; so too with our relationships. 'Relationships should not take effort': this is a belief that some people hold. They believe that they can just go into autopilot mode and cruise along in their relationship and everything will be fine. That is like buying a plant and putting it in the corner and neglecting to water or care for it. We do not want our relationships to shrivel up, so put them in care. Simple. While we receive bucket loads of positives from a healthy relationship, we definitely need to put effort in to nourish it. This nurturing ensures that you both feel connected, respected and loved. This is about clearly expressing your emotional needs and having empathetic attunement and resonance with each other, which are all important parts of healthy communication.

Think of the effort that we put into our careers. Our investment of energy in our home life often pales in comparison – and yet our home life is drastically more important than our workplace. It is often not until we have become disconnected strangers, or perhaps when we no longer know nor have influence over our children and teenagers, that we realise that we have neglected our relationships at home and allowed them to wilt and die.

Keep having fun and you'll be fine.

Just as we might learn a trade, a sport, an instrument, or a language, we need to practise and build our relationship skills. If we don't practise, we get rusty and our strengthening in that skill stops. We need to pay attention; we need to concentrate and prioritise. We build our connection, our mutual trust and our synchrony in our approach to life only through this investment of ourselves. Do we want to treat each other with lack of interest, or fuel each other's continued enjoyment of life – in this moment and in our future aspirations?

Relationships are about loving each other and having some 'in love' moments. When we are in the honeymoon phase it is all about the 'in love' feeling. This is that intoxication and excitement that we feel for each other. We can keep this fresh 'in love' enthusiasm, but only if we work to keep the relationship fresh. The key is to keep having fun together. Many couples do not have that 'in love' feeling, but they have deep connected love between them; they have attachment. The 'in love' is a beautiful experience, one to look after, but it is not the foundation of a relationship.

One way to nurture our relationships is through couple rituals. Variety and spontaneity in our lives can keep our relationships fresh, but rituals can help as well. Rituals are about creating routine time, simply windows in our day for each other, so that our days and months don't distract us from each other. We can see similar rituals with our kids, when we tuck them into bed every night; in this ritual they have our attention at the same time, in the same way, every night. They depend on this; it is a time they look to 'plug in' to their parents.

A couple ritual can be, for example, going to a nice spot in or outside of your home each day and having a drink together and comparing your days for fifteen minutes. It could be going to your couch together to say hello, or talk over an issue, or it could be going for a walk together each day at sunrise or sundown. Whatever works with your routine and whatever brings you the joy of 'plugging in' together. Rituals are the 'thing' that you do together. Jon and I go to our bed and check in when first we meet at the end of the day. In the early mornings, we have coffee and breakfast and chat together in bed. We also go for long walks with the dogs on weekends. This is our baseline; we also catch up throughout the day and have time out together at least once a week. A meal out is our favourite, but catching some live comedy is also a highlight.

When you spend this time together, **oxytocin** is released. This is the bonding hormone that tightens and fuels your connection. Togetherness time also releases oxytocin within the family unit through hugs, meals together, and sustained eye contact. This is one reason a sit-down dinner with the family is so important. It is a family ritual; it is being involved in each other's days and sharing laughs; it is an oxytocin-releasing exercise and it is *time*. This is precious time that in our future we will always wish we had spent more of and enjoyed more. Let's prevent regret here.

John Gottman is a leading researcher in marital relationships. He breaks down key predictors that he has found to indicate that a marriage will improve over the years. They include simple loving rituals such as:

1. On partings, they know something of each other's coming day.
2. On reunions, they have a low-stress reunion conversation.
3. They have affection; they touch, hold, grab and kiss, all with tenderness.
4. They have a weekly date in a relaxed atmosphere where they recharge their love batteries.
5. Each day they show appreciation and admiration for each other.

It sounds so simple, but the power of showing fondness and admiration cannot be understated. You need to nurture your relationship through attention and irreplaceability.

This is about admiring the strengths of your partner and improving the quantity and quality of the attention that you pay to them. It is about listening and engaging often and with sincerity, rather than being distracted by the pace and pressures of life, and therefore forgetting each other in the hecticness of life. This connection between you becomes your secret weapon of managing, defusing and overcoming life pressures together as a team. You come together and strengthen together as you approach life's challenges, with each other as your supportive sounding board.

Irreplaceability means that our partner is one of a kind in our eyes, and this is the absolute key to deep commitment and connection between you. If you feel that you could be replaced, then your partner's love is shallow. Is it even love? You might not naturally be good at showing love and appreciation; you may need to work at it.

NO BALANCE SHEET

Most couples who find themselves in trouble have started to create a sort of balance sheet between them. We can do this in all relationships, but it is particularly a problematic pattern with partner relationships. We can start to keep score of who is doing more for the other, and who isn't.

The problem with doing this of course is that we can then start to look for more evidence for the tally sheet. We start to *look* for the negative. We will create a negative perception bias. We can then fuel a sense of resentment and combativeness: me versus you. We can start to sit back and be in a mindset of testing each other to see if our partner really 'loves' us.

Yes, we need to be aware of our partner's behaviours, but we need to stay away from a competitive mindset that creates emotional distancing. This links to **negative attribution style** that we are about to chat about. We cannot set up hoops and choreograph how each other 'should' act. If we keep a balance sheet, we start thinking, *If he or she loves me, they will do this or that.* We set ourselves up for disappointment and that horrible, almost doomed rabbit hole of resentment and contempt.

THE GOOD BECOMES THE BAD

This is odd. Have you noticed that often the behaviour or trait that first attracted us to our partner, can actually change into something that annoys us, that we feel tension about? We start off being drawn to the positive side of this behaviour, but then we end up having to deal with the negative side of the same behaviour. We have to find a balance, a way to make it work.

For example, our partner might attract us with their exciting, fun, carefree spirit. We love that they are adventurous. But then over time we start to see this behaviour as irresponsible; we wish that they could be more of a serious adult and share the load. Or we may start off really admiring that someone is highly motivated, organised and driven. We feel that we can rely on them and we feel secure. But then in our lifestyle together we discover that we have to contend with them being too task-orientated, perhaps rigid, perhaps workaholics who can't just stop and relax. Someone who we first see as loyal and steadfast, we might come to see as dreary. We first loved how our extremely extroverted partner would walk in and own the party, but in time we may start to find them loud, overly chatty and imposing.

Basically, we have to understand that there are two sides to the same coin and we have to understand that there is the bad with the good. As with most things in life, we need to find balance. We are signing up for the full package, and we do not usually open our eyes to it fully until we are through the honeymoon phase. So not only do we need to continue to appreciate and have gratitude for their strengths, but we also need to understand and work with the flipside of their strengths. It is not until we put these challenges on the table, increase our mutual awareness and do some constructive, problem-solving talking, that we can work to find this balance.

OUR NEEDS CHANGE

When we are starting a relationship, our insecurities and our attachment fears are out there, swirling around us. Our insecurities take the lead: we fear that we are not desirable enough; we fear that we will be rejected; we fear that we will get hurt; we fear that we will screw up and embarrass ourselves. And that is only on the first date!

After we have decided that we like them, our attachment fears step in and take over. We fear whether they are really into us, whether we are their priority, whether we are emotionally safe with them and can trust them. It is an emotional minefield. What is important to know is that *this is not just you*. This is human nature and we have to wade through these fears to create a secure and safe bond.

It is not until we have consistent experiences to reassure us that our partner is really into us, that it is their absolute priority to be with us and that they will look after our hearts, that we can start to breathe out and relax. It is then that any attachment scar tissue from our past can actually start to heal by having a 'corrective' healthy relationship. We need to learn to tolerate our stages of insecurity and not to impose our desire for reassurance on the other person. We need to be patient with the time required. Otherwise we can come across as anxious and demanding. This takes a lot of emotional maturity and self-control.

TAKE YOU FOR GRANTED

Have you ever heard of the **hedonic treadmill**? If you have read Book 1 in this 'Signposts for Living' series you will have come across it. It is a fancy way of explaining that we adapt to good things and tend to eventually take them for granted. This is clearly the case with money and possessions. The more we have, the more it becomes normal to us to have them, and the more we want.

Sadly, the same is often true in our relationships. We can become spoilt brats, wanting more. It is also human nature to become complacent with what we do have. We can't do this in our relationships if we want rich, deep and fresh relationships. To avoid this trap, we cannot lose sight of the fact that our true wealth is in the richness of our relationships. We need to keep our eyes open to this side of our humanness. We can do amazing things when we feel appreciated. If we're taken for granted and we experience complacency, we lose our mojo, we lose our drive and we can become depressive. So let's stay awake, and not lose sight of how fortunate we are to have each other and to enjoy each other's love and strengths.

So many people live the cliché 'I didn't know what I had until it was gone'. Let's work to keep our relationships healthy and strong so that we don't lose them. Let's have our eyes open to what we have now!

CHAPTER 7
POSITIVE – NEGATIVE ATTRIBUTION STYLE

The brain is fascinating. The health and stage of our relationship dramatically shapes whether we can see or are blind to our partner's behaviour. This is crazy and bizarre and, as always, it is a smart thing to know how the brain machine is working so you can catch yourself when you are unbalanced, so that you can regain some control and steer yourself towards a more balanced, rational world.

Our **positive and negative attribution styles** are the lens through which we see our partner (and others). We create a bias that means we can't see their behaviour in a neutral and more accurate way. We are either using rose-coloured glasses and are in fantasy mode, or we are using black-lens glasses and can only see their bad behaviours and traits. By learning about attribution style we can know when we are doing this and work to bring ourselves back to the middle. We can then be more neutral and use a clear lens so that the accurate – good *and* bad – picture can be seen. It's then that we can appreciate and work with the truth.

We are blind in love and hate. The most peculiar thing about attribution style is that we only see what we expect to see, and we don't see the opposite. So in an overly positive relationship phase, we only see the positive behaviours from our partner and we literally don't see many of the negative. When in a negative phase in a relationship, we don't see the positive, and we are like vultures circling for the negative, ready to spot those behaviours. If we do see a positive – if this sunlight creeps through – we will work to dismiss it.

POSITIVE ATTRIBUTION STYLE HONEYMOON PHASE	NEGATIVE ATTRIBUTION STYLE COUPLES IN CRISIS

POSITIVE BEHAVIOURS

'He is so thoughtful'

'I can rely on her'

'He is a great father'

'She's really good at …'

###

'That was a fluke'

'That's only one positive thing amongst the huge pile of negative'

'What's in it for him?'

☹ NEGATIVE BEHAVIOURS

'She didn't mean it'

'It's not his fault'

'She's just having a bad day'

'He's just stressed'

'Today you annoyed me'

😠 NEGATIVE BEHAVIOURS

'She always nags'

'He never has time for me'

'He's always critical'

'She's only in it for herself'

POSITIVE ATTRIBUTION STYLE

If we are in a healthy place with our partner or are in the honeymoon phase, it is likely that we will have a positive bias towards them. This is the positive attribution style. We will look for and see their positive behaviours and we will be blind to or dismiss their negative behaviours. We will explain their positive behaviours as being due to their positive personality traits and we will make broad positive interpretations. We explain our partner's positive behaviours as permanent strengths, and see them as having permanent positive personality traits and abilities, while we see their negative behaviours as just the changing mood or current stressors that will pass. When we are in the honeymoon phase, we really have rose-coloured glasses on, to the point that we are quite unbalanced in what we see in our partner and how generously we attribute all good things to them (many things no one else sees because they are not looking so hard, or because we have actually projected these positives onto our partner).

When negative behaviours do manage to come into our line of vision, positive attribution style will cause us to dismiss their behaviour as a once-off, not their fault or only an accident. At most we will keep the focus of the negative behaviour as the current issue; we won't generalise or make big negative character statements. We will use the softer timeframe terms of 'sometimes' and 'lately' – for example, 'You haven't had time for me lately'.

NEGATIVE ATTRIBUTION STYLE

If our relationship is unhappy and conflict-ridden then we are likely to be in a negative attribution style. We then expect more of the negative behaviours that we have been experiencing. We see them everywhere, and each one just provides more evidence that our partner has bad character flaws and bad intent. We see their problem areas as permanent and make 'always' and 'never' black-and-white statements about them. We won't see or believe their positive behaviour; we tend to dismiss or not trust it. We search for and churn over negative behaviours. If couples actually separate, then the negative attribution style becomes complete. We can start to demonise our ex. We can rewrite history to completely dismiss our ex's positives. Our view becomes one-sided as we only focus on and see the negatives, and are busy making lots of generalised interpretations such as, 'He always did this …', or, 'It was her personality to do that …'

Another way to think about attributional style is our level of hope. The art of hope in our relationship is about finding permanent and personality causes for our partner's good behaviour and temporary and non-personal causes for their negative behaviour. The opposite pattern exists for despair. Our degree of hope is directly linked up with the selective attention that is core to attribution style.

When you are in relationship crisis, perhaps there are patterns of behaviour between you and your partner that really aren't healthy. Perhaps you are doing harm to each other, or you are in a stressful time and, instead of pulling together, you are pulling apart. For example, if you have been distracted by life, work stressors or parenting stressors, or you have become lost in chasing your to-do list, then you can become a tuned-out version of yourselves that is irritable, absent and reactive. Or perhaps you have a new chapter in your life – new studies, new work, new baby – and with these big changes, you have forgotten each other; you are neglecting each other and your relationship. Whatever the cause, when we are in a negative space like this, we can be tempted to see our partner with a negative attribution style. We don't even see the positives that they do for us. We don't notice that they have filled the car with fuel for us, or that we have come home to a cooked meal. We might not see that they have done the dishes at night because that is *our* preference, when they really would have preferred to do the dishes in the morning. We don't notice their questions about how our day was, or the fact that they are there for us if we want to talk through what is stressing us. Instead, we have a negative head, so we are only scanning and seeing negative behaviours. We see that they have left making the lunches to us, that they are home later than they had said they'd be, that they keep nagging us, that they fuss over small things. We are blind to the good, and search for and launch at the bad.

It is important to monitor the health of our relationship and to monitor what we are doing with our attribution style. Obviously, our attribution style – how positive or negative we expect our partner to be – is going to colour our experience of our partner and shape our behaviour enormously. Our perceptions will influence our reactions, which can in turn make a situation much better or much worse. When we stay with a positive attribution style, we get to actually notice and experience our partner's generous and positive behaviours. This allows us to have gratitude and appreciation, which is not only good for our mental health, but it naturally fuels more positive behaviour from our partner.

We can do amazing things when we are appreciated. If we are not appreciated, we become disheartened and hurt, and we can give up. So even when your partner does something that annoys you, examine which explanation is accurate – is it a specific explanation such as 'She is tired', 'He is stressed', 'She is in a bad mood', or a general explanation like 'She is always a pain', 'He never pays attention', 'She doesn't care about me'? When your partner does something positive, then really acknowledge it and, where accurate, look for general explanations – things you can attribute to them like 'He's very generous', 'She is very caring', 'She is reliable'. With positive behaviours, try to avoid dismissing them as one-off ('That was just luck', or 'She must want something').

As much as we want to be aware of our *interpretations* of our partners' behaviour, sometimes our partners really *do* have a consistent cluster of negative behaviours. They may be consistently selfish, unreasonable, manipulative or prone to drama. When you've experimented with whether you are being unbalanced in your interpretation, but a very clear pattern continues, then of course you need to be realistic about these significant problems. Positive or negative attribution style is more about daily issues that are mild and irritating. Awareness of attribution style is *not* about compromising on or allowing clearly abusive or neglectful behaviours. You always need to look after yourself and keep yourself psychologically safe and healthy.

When we feel that we are living well and that we are living towards our ideals, then we feel gratification because our highest strengths are being realised. When our partner has positive attribution towards us, they can see these positive behaviours in us. We feel validated and we are encouraged to continue with our positive choices and mindful behaviour. There is astonishing research that shows that this dance of partners seeing and appreciating these positives in each other's behaviour is perhaps one of the strongest predictors of stable and happy relationships. The key ingredient here is not the degree of the *actual* positive partner behaviour, but the degree to which the partners *perceive* each other to have these behaviours. It is about our *perception* of our partner – our positive expectations of them.

This links up with the research on the profound effects of gratitude. Satisfied couples see strengths and virtues in their partners that outsiders do not necessarily see. In contrast, dissatisfied couples have an image of each other that is negatively tainted. Positive attributions are self-fulfilling because the partners are motivated to live up to their idealised views of each other. Also, they have a buffer in that they don't really observe, absorb or read too much into daily hassles and daily transgressions. When the negative issues do become more apparent, they approach the conflict with a more generous heart, or downplay it and are able to forgive each other more easily. We really need to work to grab the reins and remain as rational as possible during our honeymoon phase, and we need to ground ourselves with a more balanced and appreciative view during times of relationship stress. At least we can understand what is happening to us with our attribution style. That is a solid start.

CHAPTER 8
HEALTHY RELATIONSHIPS: KNOW THE SKILLS

We have figured out a lot with regard to communication skills and relationship building. So let's harness this knowledge and use it to help our relationships thrive. Healthy relationships require self-awareness, awareness of our interactions, and mindful communication and listening. When we are on track with this approach to life, the return for this investment is truly profound. We draw people to us, we help them grow as our relationship nurtures them, and we can enjoy the most beautiful expression of them as they feel safe with us. When we feel understood and connected, our reactivity is kept at bay. We can remain open to others and not in avoidant or fighting back mode. If you want a beautiful home, you create and tend to it. If you want a thriving career, you invest actively in it. So too with our relationships.

It is one thing to learn to meet our people and to let them into our hearts and our worlds, but it is another to keep our heart open to them in our day-to-day moments together. We all need to remember to remain playful and creative in nurturing and fuelling our relationships. We need to get busy caring for ourselves and caring for our relationships, with our eyes, ears and smiles open. It is so easy to feel disconnected and defensive with others. It is so easy to become distracted and absorbed by our own worries, that we can start to think with separateness rather than connectedness. A mindful mind – being awake to the moment – is the key to thriving relationships as well as our own mental health.

COMMUNICATION AND DISAGREEMENTS

Relationship breakdowns do not actually happen over the issues causing a conflict, but more often due to the damaging way that we communicate about these issues, how we speak with and treat each other. Communication is about investigating the other person's perspective.

I mean communication with partners, family, children, friends, work colleagues – anyone, really. The main ingredients are listening and learning about the other, so that you can understand where the other one is coming from. If both people do this then they are working to build a bridge between where they both stand.

Communication means investigating another's perspective.

We have all experienced communication that has made us feel loved, respected and connected, and many interactions that have left us feeling hurt, frustrated, annoyed, disregarded and disconnected.

When we're in a negative interaction, we try to avoid this experience of being stressed and threatened; we may shut down, stop listening, or hold back from sharing ourselves. We also can become very negative towards the other person, we can react with judgement and blame towards them, and we can make gross generalisations like 'They're a moron, they're horrible', which sets us up to just spiral down in our interactions with them even more. We are in defensive mode and are critical. There is not much intelligent understanding of them going on here and not much room for empathy and compassion. Our views can then become more fixed, and we can create a fearful set against them, growing rigid in our feelings and views of them. We have negatively pigeonholed them.

For example, I often say to student clients, 'Play it smart; make sure your teachers like you. Don't suck up, but know that they are human, and you will get the best out of them if they like you, and the worst out of them if they think negatively about you. Set yourself up for a smooth year. Don't load up the teacher with a negative view of you. They will have tired, exhausted days, and their human bias will come out against you. Play it smart.' Sounds calculated, but it is only intelligent. It is understanding the nature of key people in your life, and human fallibility.

Fortunately, we can take control of our communication skills and, by cultivating our interpersonal capacity, we can nurture our relationships. As you bring mindfulness to your communication, as you pay attention to your sensations, thoughts, and feelings, you will increase your ability to respond *intentionally* to other people rather than *habitually* just reacting. Communication is about connecting with others, using our bodies and our minds, non-verbally and verbally.

I'M READING YOU, YOUR NON-VERBALS

Strangely, when we think about talking with someone or recalling a conversation, we focus on what is said. We say, 'They said this, I said that', but we really miss the point here, the true reality. The *words* are the minority of what is going on. The majority of information that we receive from each other is via **non-verbal communication**: our tone of voice, our posture, our facial expressions.

Our body language is therefore crucial and it needs to convey that we are approachable and welcoming. Often, however, our body language is saying that we are more like an impenetrable brick wall, or that we are a scared mouse, or that we are coming at them with guns loaded, ready to launch an attack. It is our body language (voice, face, posture, eye contact, gestures) that shapes how others receive our communication. It is much less the words that we use. It is really interesting that in session at work, I can make a fairly accurate assessment of how a client is travelling, how they feel about being in session and the interpersonal dynamic between a couple, just by observing their non-verbal cues.

Words are completely in the background. Yet when we plan a conversation, we focus on the words we will use, and when we recount a conversation it is mostly the words that we reflect upon. We actually need to think about the massive role of our non-verbals in our communication equation. Look at yourself, look at your body language. What are you saying to the other person? How are you shaping the communication through your non-verbals? When we communicate, we want to keep the other person's defences down. We want to be talking to their good side, their softer, more open and accepting side, not their defensive side. We all have both sides to us. We want to keep our ears open and stay in constructive mode, not destructive mode.

Teenagers get a really bad rap partly because of their body language. They walk around in their own worlds. They like to have their headphones in, they often have poor eye contact, and commonly hide behind their caps or hair and walk with their heads down. It is a rare thing for a teenager to walk with their head up, jawline out, watching the horizon or what is going on around them. Teenagers typically like to spend large stretches of time in their caves. They need their own space, ideally their own bedrooms, where they can hide away and be in their own headspace. Of course, we adults gently get them out for some interaction and sunlight because it is good for them, but we need to appreciate that retreat into a teenage cave is a developmentally normal stage. So when a teenager is walking around with their closed-off body language, they are often projecting this distancing technique – going into their cave.

How does the rest of the world perceive this body language? They think that teenagers are shut down, perhaps rude, have 'attitude' or are being defiant. This is accentuated enormously when teens are in a group, and they are all looking shut down and even broody. But all they are doing is being teenagers. Give them time; they will come out of their caves and become more interactive with the broader world. It is crucial to understand them and not to judge. They are child adults; they need patience and support.

At work, I am very mindful of my body language when I meet clients for the first time. I have to balance being open, friendly and relaxed with carrying enough authority to generate their confidence in me. I can read that some clients need more of a relaxed experience from me, while others need a more professional tone in my body language to help them feel calm and confident. It is not really what I say but what I do that creates a solid foundation for our ongoing therapeutic relationship.

If you enjoy people-watching, then you are already practising observing body language. Whether you are sitting at a bar, café, or airport, scanning the people around you out of vague interest, you are observing body language. You cannot hear their conversation, you do not have their verbals, just their non-verbals, to go by. Sure, you are looking at their presentation, but how long would you watch if it was just a photo in front of you? Not for long; you would get bored, as the information is flat and static. With people-watching, you are observing and reading their non-verbal language.

Now we need to flip it and monitor our *own* non-verbal language.

STOP THE SAME PROBLEMS REPEATING, SORT THEM OUT

If we had a business, we would routinely review how the business is going. We would look for areas of strength and where there are problems, and where we can refine and improve. We would look for areas of future growth and expansion, and review the culture and the morale within the business. We would put the issues on the table and make quality time to look through everything, understand the issues, communicate clearly, make a plan, find the resources needed, and regularly review our progress. This is all very sensible and key to running a smooth and successful business. Do we do this in our relationships? Seldom. Yet this is exactly what we need to do to keep our relationships healthy and thriving.

A reality in most relationships, however, is that we often do not stop and reflect on what our problem areas are. We don't communicate effectively about them, we don't actively listen to each other, and we expect the other person to read our minds and know what our problems are. We go around and around in circles, not effectively addressing problem areas and not understanding or actioning our needs and future goals. What we are doing is not working and yet we just keep doing it. Around and around, almost banging our head against a wall, getting no outcome, so we keep banging.

Do you take on a victim mindset? Do you blame the other person? Is your mind shut off to learning about yourself? If it hurts you to take responsibility, then you are in trouble. To communicate effectively we must learn about our role, and learn about our partner's needs and how we are affecting them. Effective communication is about stepping up and owning change.

If it is not working – if our avoidance, our ignoring, our aimless talking is not working – then we need to change our approach and find an approach that does work. Before we go further, there are two big exceptions to this proactive approach. First of all, jump forward to Chapter 21 of this book, which works through the issue of tricky people. Unfortunately, some of us have people in our lives who do not intend to be constructive, want to address issues, or want to live well. Instead these tricky people's agenda is to destroy. They want power over the other person and they want to damage and undermine the other person's voice. If you are working with a person who is intentionally destructive, then you cannot work through issues with them, because they don't want to work through these issues. You are left instead with the need for boundaries and self-protection.

The other exception is if there has been a lot of damage and hurt from one to another. If this is the case, the question is whether the attachment bond is still there and whether there is a desire to recover and rebuild – or if there is a desire to not be with that person. This is confronting, but is often a reality.

When we do continue to feel attachment and desire for a future together, if there is a history of damage and hurt, we are still going to be in our corners, avoidant of further hurt. We will have learnt that we cannot trust that person with our heart and our vulnerability, and we are going to need to see consistent evidence of good intention to reassess and find them trustworthy. *They need to become worthy of our trust again.* The problem is not that we have 'trust issues'; the problem is that the person has proven they are not trustworthy. When recovering from hurt, we need to respect the time and the pace it takes to rebuild this trust, our bond and our ability to be light and playful together. We need to feel safe so we can come out from our corner.

The bottom line is that to address problem issues in our relationship and to work towards launching into our future, we need to feel hopeful about our relationship potential and our future together. This takes trust. So if we have a wounded party, we need to slow it down and respect that it will take time and consistently healthy behaviour to enable the relationship to recover.

Here are some ideas to constructively address issues. Let's get them sorted.

1. Set a time to talk through issues. You must prioritise a time. Perhaps you can do this spontaneously, but if you are not getting around to it, or find that you are being avoidant, then setting a time once a week could be a good idea. Make it a quality time when you are not tired and you have few distractions (like kids).

2. Set an agenda. Put up a piece of paper on the cupboard door, with a line drawn down the middle. Each of you has a column to list hot issues that you want to work through. These are issues that it would make you feel calmer and more content to have addressed. Alternatively list desires you want to brainstorm. Add to the list as you think of things that would be helpful to talk through.

3. During your talk time, pick one agenda item from each of the lists. The list is a working document. You gradually work through the issues, crossing them off as you go, and adding issues as they come up. You can see each other's agenda, which gives you both

preparation time and allows you to become more mindful of the issue in the interim. Who knows? With your more mindful response to the issue on the list yet to be covered, you may even resolve the issue.

4. The list is for big issues: issues that keep recurring or issues that have a lot of meaning to you.

5. Your job is to investigate each other's opinions on the issues first (see communication chapter). It is not until you are truly experts on each other's perspective that you can work towards a solution.

6. Use the talking stone if one or both of you feel it is needed (see below).

7. Of course, it is important to try not to use any negative gestures or facial expressions. Stay mindful of this and practise open listening and curious body language.

8. Write down brainstormed options, and work out pros and cons. Share your opinion of the best option and if you have differing opinions, slow it down. You do not have to decide then and there. Keep massaging and brainstorming options until you find a win:win. This is a very creative process.

9. The exception is if an issue is extremely important to one partner and less so to the other. On these occasions there may be a gift of generosity to go with the

other partner's perspective because it is important to him/her (although you cannot do this consistently; otherwise there will be an imbalance in outcome in favour of one partner). Alternatively, partners can trade. Partner 1 has his burning issue, partner 2 has her burning issue, so they decide to be mutually generous and agree with each other's requests for their relevant issues.

10. Care about each other. This is not about winning. This is about both of you being important, and while you need to advocate for yourself, you also need to really, *really* care about how your partner is experiencing the issue. You both have a 50% vote; value it.

TALKING STONE

The talking stone is an age-old technique that we use to slow our conversation down, to increase equality in the amount of talking time between partners, and to emphasise listening. You can use any object to pass between you (ball, pen, cup?). It is about taking turns and learning not to interrupt. It is also about noticing who has had the stone more. If you find you've had a long way from 50% talking time each, then this is not okay; one of you needs to learn to speak more concisely and for less time, and the other needs to learn to speak up more. The emphasis is about finding more balance.

Once there is a clear issue to talk through, one person starts holding the stone and it is their turn to talk. The other person cannot interrupt, only listen. Then when the person has finished talking, they pass the stone to the other person for their turn to talk, and the dance continues, to and fro, to and fro. This really is a great technique, particularly when the conversation has often been dominated by one party, or when there is a lot of talking over each other and butting in.

Of course, there is the challenge of staying calm and keeping our communication constructive. When couples are in conflict and disconnected, almost every conflict can become volatile and explosive. Even couples who are in a good space together will have sensitive issues that can rise to conflict. When we are provoked, we want to give as good as we get, but this does not solve the problem; it just exacerbates into further conflict because the other person is also busy giving as good as they get. And then the conflict dance continues.

The key to remaining constructive is having a soft-mannered approach. This quieter voice and this controlled language keeps us on topic, reduces the hostility and therefore works to keep their defensive walls and our defensive walls down. You can even discuss each person's prioritising of the problem and reluctance to put in energy. You need to work with the person, not the other person's brick wall. That is why you need to approach the conversation with compassion and camaraderie. Walk alongside each other while talking about the problem. This is much more useful than being in conflict, going head to head, where you have lost each other's good intention and both of you are functioning from flight/fright/freeze mode. In this crisis mode your executive functioning (your clever frontal lobe) is not being used.

Here lies the truth: the best way of winning an argument is not to have an argument at all.

COLLABORATIVE NOT COMPETITIVE

The essence of addressing issues is that we need to be cooperative and collaborative, not competitive. Couples come along to therapy usually at a point where it is long overdue and their relationship is on life support. There are common themes. These include an imbalance in power, conflict over domestic issues, family, children, money and sex. The most encompassing theme, however, is an erosion of respect for one another and feeling as if needs and expectations are not being met.

The goal is to constructively resolve problems, not to punish each other. If you are wanting to vent and punish the other, then this is not communication; this is doing harm. It's purely destructive. Unfortunately, when we become hurt, and we are in our corner with our defensive walls up, we do routinely become competitive on some level. We shift to thinking and behaving as if it's us versus them. The goal is to regulate our emotional state, to rationalise our thinking, to calm down. Hopefully, while we are in our corners, we do not harm the other person, because this of course would not only distract from the original issue, but it would create more hurt, more walls, and more competitiveness.

As mentioned earlier, some tricky people have a competitive outlook and approach as their normal starting point, not just as a defensive reaction. This competitive trait is a very significant problem and reduces the probability of ever being able to find a healthy relationship. You cannot get a relationship healthy on your own. It takes two, and if one person does not want to find a collaborative and mindful outcome, then your hands are tied.

A constructive approach incorporates genuine empathy for each other, making us feel that our hurt is heard and apologised for. This allows us to move towards releasing and healing.

YOU CHANGE FIRST

A lovely and courageous gift that you can give to others is, instead of waiting for the other person to change, you go first. You change first. Like petulant children, we are inclined to sit back and say, 'But she is not doing this', or, 'He is not doing that'. Because our partner is misbehaving or not improving, we feel justified in not acting well ourselves. This is ridiculous. Of course, while it might occasionally spring from laziness or stubbornness on our part, it is usually due to fear. We fear putting ourselves forward and being vulnerable if *they* are not going to also do their part to nurture the relationship and address problem issues. It is very wise to go first, however. Take the lead. Put in some good faith. You cannot ask of others what you are not first asking of yourself. Wise and true. You will feel proud of your mature 'adulting' if you go first.

WARN OF YOUR HOT TOPICS

When we have a 'hot' issue, it is a really good idea to label it and communicate this to each other. We are saying, 'Please be careful with me, because I am loaded on this one.' If a couple is having difficulties talking through these hot topics, it is crucial to use these skills so that you are careful with each other, so that you do not harm each other and so that you can resolve the issues and give more peace and support to the vulnerable partner.

THIRD PARTY TEMPTATION

A very common theme of marital conflict is a longing for excitement. We have prescribed to the traditional system, we have secure jobs, we own our own homes, we are in a committed relationship and we have kids. But we feel discontent. We feel lost. Setting out in life, these were our goals, but now we feel burdened or on the merry-go-round of life. We become irritable and reactive, and we withdraw. The intimacy in the relationship has gone stale and we feel physically alone. Our sense of ourselves as sexual beings feels distant; we don't feel sexually confident or desirable.

Instead of looking at this situation with analytical and creative eyes, we stay too close to it; we spiral downwards without reflective thought. We are in danger of having an affair. The novelty, the exhilaration of the chase, the honeymoon phase revisited: we experience this option as a break from life's complications (the complete opposite to the reality that follows). We may think we have missed out on life experiences due to the path we took. What about other life paths? We ask, 'Is there more out there than I have experienced?' We want to feel desired and we want excitement.

If you are open to attraction to others and from others, this is information that you are not in a good place in your relationship. It is a long overdue wake-up call to stop and get healthy at home. To re-orientate, wake up and refuel your marital relationship and your relationship with life.

We need courage to address issues in our relationships. To push our relationships out of their usual mould and stay fresh in our efforts to find meaning and happiness.

'I' VERSUS 'YOU'

This sounds so clichéd, but it is true and worth its salt. Use 'I' statements, not 'you' statements. When we use 'I' statements we are keeping our focus on how we have been affected, on how we feel, on our perception. When we use 'you' statements we can sound attacking and persecutory, and we can easily get the other person's back up. It's understandable that in this situation they feel defensive and come back at us. So rather than saying, 'You don't care about me, you only wanted to impress everyone else by getting them a drink,' say instead, 'I felt really upset when you got everyone else a drink but me'.

And remember that '*I* think you are selfish' and '*I* think you are lazy' are not helpful 'I' statements! They are examples of useless and damaging name calling. We are not in primary school. These are dangerous generalisations, full of negative attribution style, or bias. Your partner will also feel like you have thrown your good opinion of them away for good.

Be succinct with your words; do not ramble on. Do not hammer in and repeat your point over and over. This does not make your point heard; it's just venting your emotion. This is punishing your partner and they will just tune out. You have their attention for a certain amount of time, and you value their time, so think about how to speak succinctly and efficiently, always with the bigger, intended outcome in mind.

MIXED SOLUTIONS

Life can be very complex. Our quandaries are not simple and are often not easily resolved. Sometimes there is no clear way of seeing through to a solution. Life is also often full of dilemmas; there is no clear right or wrong and there are layered consequences. Often we are choosing 'the better of two evils' rather than a completely positive solution.

Part of becoming an advanced adult is the ability to negotiate through these uncertainties in life, some of them dilemmas, where there are not clear answers. The key is to contemplate the options with a calm mind, to work through them, so that at minimum you know that you have thought through your options thoroughly. This means allowing options to remain in your awareness before you launch into forming an opinion. This is respecting the decision-making process rather than forcing a decision just to avoid the unsettled feeling we get when no decision has been made. Your mind needs to keep having the conversation until it eventually finds a resolution, a 'best fit' solution. Often we can think laterally and come up with a new, third option. What is important is to accept that as adults we will feel ambiguity, we will hold opinions and have emotional experiences that contradict each other's but are valid, nevertheless.

It is important that we avoid developing an either/or mindset to life, because life is not simple.

INTENTIONS

When looking at ongoing conflict, it is important to take a moment and look at your intentions and your partner's intentions and your willingness for change. What do you want? Do your behaviours match up with your intentions and what you want?

You may be very hurt, wary and in your shell. You might, however, gauge that your partner has good intentions and is also lost. It's useful to behave as if you are in repairing mode, putting good intent into your actions and working towards healing. You do not have the luxury of staying in your shell waiting to come out when you feel safer. If you do this, the problems will continue. To progress you need to venture forward and put in *your* half of shifting the dynamic, or modify your behaviour so that it is healthy and healing.

So many couples just behave the same way over and over again and they keep getting the same deteriorating results. What they are doing communication-wise in their relationship is not working, but they just keep doing it anyway. They don't try an alternative skill set or work to increase their insight about the situation. They just keep sinking the marriage ship further. You can keep banging your head against the wall and compounding your pain, or you can learn a different and healthier approach. It's your choice.

ESSENTIAL TO DISAGREE

It is absolutely critical that we attend to our relationships if we want them to be vibrant and to flourish. Disagreements are essential in relationships, but this does not mean destructive conflict. If you do not disagree, then you are not voicing your own needs and you are not engaging; you are deferring to the other person. Unless you have a difference of opinion then you are not being your own person with your own mind.

If we do not know what bothers each other, we do not have the opportunity to reduce the inevitable tensions that arise whenever you put two people together. Unless we invest energy in our relationships, conflicts are inevitable, even if they are never spoken of. Any two individuals are different creatures with different needs and approaches and their own unique goals. Without effective communication, these differences can turn into problem areas and can become amplified. Interpersonal mindfulness is our protection during strained and difficult times; it can help us work to prevent relationships falling apart.

DESTRUCTIVE BEHAVIOUR WITH OUR LOVED ONES

We commonly treat our loved ones the worst. With them, we can often be the harshest version of ourselves. People state that they want a healthy, enjoyable relationship, yet the ugly truth is that if you were to see into many people's lives, you'd see that the person they treat the worst in the world is their partner. It is not uncommon for people to treat their partner atrociously, while being much more respectful and considerate of others in their lives. Some people even have a verbally and psychologically cruel and abusive approach towards their loved ones, and neglect their emotional or functional needs. At the same time as saying that they want a strong and intimate relationship, they might actually be smashing it down or withdrawing all of the ingredients that could mend it.

While there is a background to this damaging behaviour, and it's usually a case of acting out from frustration and insecurity, the sheer lack of common sense to this day-to-day behaviour is extraordinary. All too often, people lash out at their loved partner until one day their partner turns around and says, 'I can't take this anymore. I want out.' They are then often left with shock, regret and an earnest desire to change. Often it is too late, for the threads of the relationship have been severed.

This is the same for our relationships with our children, our families and our work colleagues. It is not so much the case with friendships, as we are less complacent with friendships. We understand that if we step over the line, our friend will disconnect from us. So here we are wanting a close positive relationship with our partner, a positive, constructive workplace, and open communication with our teenager, but our actions do not reflect our intentions. The truth is, many of us are asleep when it comes to the true state of our destructive behaviours in our relationships. The partner/s then of course become hyperaware and on the lookout for the next attack. Even if they are small jibes, they are still actions intent on hurting others. We might hide behind old habits or justifications like 'That's just what we do', or 'That's just Roger!' We do not realise that we are sabotaging the healthy relationships that we actually want

CRITICAL BOSSY

It can be very confronting to think honestly about the percentage of time we spend being critical or directive – bossy, to put it bluntly – in our personal lives. Our closest relationships can become power struggles.

Think about it: how do *you* react when a bossy person tells you what to do? We usually feel resistance and respond with a 'Get stuffed' reaction. We often feel resentment, frustration, and don't feel like complying. Perhaps we are then overt in our refusal, or we are passive-aggressive, saying, 'I forgot' because we are not comfortable with being honest and upfront.

I sometimes ask people, 'What would happen if every time you said something negative, you received an electric zap?' Their response is, 'Well I would be pretty silent!' Precisely. We need to turn this negative tendency on its head. We don't like hearing a negative and critical tone from others, so why are we so negative, critical or bossy with our people? Why do we use critical 'humour' with them? It makes no sense.

Do critical people come from critical families? Usually. Negativity, pessimism and bitchiness are also traits that are often learnt from family cultures. The question is, do we want to continue these legacies into our futures? Probably not! We need to envision a different way of interacting with the people in our lives. We need to change long-standing habits, even when it is easier to just keep doing what we have always done. It is too easy to continue with our bad habits of communication, even when this is not working for us and we are hurting the people that we love.

WORD GRENADES

Words can be so powerful. Words can be so harmful. Yet when we are distressed, we shoot from the hip, throw word grenades and actually try to think of the most hurtful words to use. It's purposeful. We don't think about the long-term damage, we just think about winning the power struggle in the now. We want to create hurt *now*, because we ourselves are hurting. Unfortunately, these cruel words usually become tattooed into the other person's mind and they can cause long-term damage. We need to tread very cautiously with each other's hearts; we need to think about the blast damage from our hurtful word grenades.

IN YOUR CORNER

We have fairly universal emotional needs. We need to be treated with kindness. We need our people to listen to us and have patience and tolerance towards us. It makes sense that if we want to be treated in this way, we need to cultivate these qualities ourselves and apply them in our treatment of others.

The core of every relationship is trust. Is this person in your corner? Do they have your best interests as their priority? Do they have a value system that ensures they do the right thing by you even when there are no eyes on them? Do they have good intentions? Are they a trustworthy person? It is through our daily interactions that we demonstrate to each other that we are indeed trustworthy, that we are safe to be vulnerable with each other.

Within our relationships, especially as parent role models to our children, we need to live together with kindness, tolerance, and ever-improving skills in conflict resolution. It takes courage to engage in peacemaking and constructive resolution; it takes impulsivity and immaturity to verbally attack each other. We need to break out of our habitual reactions to stressful, emotional and threatening interaction. Our motto needs to be 'Do no harm', especially to people we love.

CULTIVATING INTERPERSONAL MINDFULNESS

How do we dramatically improve our relationships through cultivating interpersonal mindfulness? If you can master these four skills, you are miles ahead and definitely at the interpersonal masterclass level! They are Openness, Equanimity, Empathy and Sympathetic Joy.

- **Openness** is how prepared we are to see others with an open heart and mind. We need to be open to seeing the situation from the other person's perspective.

- **Equanimity** is realising and celebrating that all relationships have inherent value. We all deserve to be treated with consideration. We all simply want and need love and kindness. There is a bucket of wisdom here. This is about a settling and maturity in your own mind. It means learning about interconnectedness, composure and balance in life.

- **Empathy** is the ability to identify with another's feelings. This is putting yourself in another's shoes and feeling around, relating to their experience. Some people intuitively feel for others; they are natural empathisers. Others may need to practise by asking the inflicted person what happened and listening, *really* listening, trying to imagine what they might feel like. We all want to be accepted, to feel secure and to feel loved. Empathy is about tapping into the other person's vulnerable moments when they are feeling insecure.

- **Sympathetic joy** is about wanting the other person to experience happiness and joy, and celebrating and delighting in it when they do.

DOUBLE NEGATIVES

There is a good reason to avoid double negatives I've intentionally flagged this throughout this series as it is such a damaging habit. Using double negatives affects our own self-talk, our communication with others and our absent-minded parenting.

Do you recall the pink rabbit mentioned in Book 1, Chapters 24 and 31? (If we think *don't think of a pink rabbit*, we *will* think of a pink rabbit before we can move away from this thought.) A double negative statement is when we use two negative statements, thinking that they cancel each other out and create a positive statement. But the problem is that this intention does not actually work. All we hear and all that our brains really compute is the negative. Australians are especially prone to using double negative statements; unfortunately it seems to be core to our culture. Here in Australia we tend to say 'not bad' rather than 'good'; we say 'she doesn't do a bad job' rather than 'she does a great job'. It seems to pain us to make a direct, positive statement.

My most shocking example was in session when a husband, intending to compliment his wife, said, 'You're not unattractive.' He was trying to tell her that she looked attractive, but all she heard was 'unattractive'! Why? Because with double negative statements, the brain taps into the negative statement first before it can then work to disagree with it. All we are doing is reinforcing the negative statement. If we hear, 'It's not going to storm', we think about 'storm', not clear blue skies. If we see a sign 'Don't touch the wet paint', yep you've got it, all we are thinking about is touching the wet paint. Another favourite are the signs that say, 'Don't step in the garden'. I wasn't thinking about stepping in the garden, but now I am!

The takeaway message here is use positive statements and try to avoid double negative statements. A double negative does not equal a positive statement; it equals just a negative statement that we are left working to get away from. Know how your human brain works and don't let it work against you.

OTHERS' RIGHT TO BE WRONG

Okay, get your head around this. Other people have the right to be wrong.

We hold our opinions because we think they are correct. When other people hold a different or opposing opinion, then by logic we think that their opinion is wrong. We need to grasp that it is okay for them to have a different opinion, to have a different understanding from us, which by deduction means that they have the right to be wrong.

Firstly, they are their own person and have a right to their own opinion. We are not dictators, they are not our minions, and we are not perfect. Many times, others will be proven to be correct while we are not. We are not robots or computers; we are humans, learning machines, who get a lot wrong on our way to (hopefully) getting more and more right. If we find others to be irrational or ignorant, it is not our job to correct them. Many, however, strangely feel they have a right or even an obligation to go around banging everyone else on the head with their own opinions, with what they believe to be the truth, because it is *their* truth. This is really disrespecting the reality that others have the right to their own opinions, even if it seems wrong to us.

I hear many, many comments that I find (from my perspective) ignorant. However, it is not my place to impose my contrasting view. If I feel like having the conversation and it is a safe space, I could float my opposing view for their consideration, but if not, I will gently sidestep and leave them be; it is their world.

The other issue is that even when you put your opinion forward, you cannot make someone else take it on board. They may be open to hearing the perspective, or they might not. It is information for them to do with as they choose. A bit like 'You can bring a horse to water, but you can't make it drink'. People need to have their ears open if they are to change, to learn and to expand their understanding. So even if you share, it has to be with no expectation. You cannot be led by your ego, which makes you feel a *need to be right* – which is often the real issue in the room. If you are needing to be right, then it is not the controversial issue we are even talking about, it is your vulnerable ego.

Leave your ego at the door.

There are exceptions of course, such as when a moral line has been crossed over or when abuse is being carried out towards an individual, a group, animals, society or the environment. These moral violations require us to take a stand, obviously guarding our own safety when holding moral violators to account. But again, on these occasions sadly we need to realise that we cannot change a person's perspective unless they are open to expansion. If they are stuck in their moral ignorance, your impact will be limited. The actual event here is that you are showing them that you are not going to tolerate that behaviour in your earshot.

NEED FOR COMPARTMENTALISATION

Compartmentalisation: the work me, the parent me, the partner me, the friend me; different environments require different things from us. At work we need to be efficient and task-driver, at home and with our people, we need to be more relaxed and focused on relationships. It is a skill to balance our different worlds. It is necessary to have boundaries for different areas of our lives, so that one does not flow over and monopolise another. For example, we need to learn to leave our work stress at work so that we can recharge at home and be available to our loved ones. When we are stressed by home life, we need to be professional with our boundaries and do our best to leave our personal life out of work. This, fortuitously, can actually give us a break from thinking about our personal problems 24/7.

Different roles require different priorities and different attitudes. We cannot just be goal directed at home; we need to be sharing and collaborative. We cannot be purely relationship orientated at work; we need to show independence, initiative and task orientation. Many clients have told their partners that they don't want them home until they have got their head out of work mode, because they don't want to be on the receiving end of their work stress.

A lovely approach is to do something to create a clear change in your mindset from work to home mode. This has been called creating your **'third space'**. It is an activity that you stop off to do as you transition from your work self to your home self. It is de-stressing. Either stop at a park on the way home and read a few pages of a book or listen to a non-work-related podcast in the car on the way home. The key is to do some *other* thing that de-stresses you, so you can shortwire the stress momentum of work in your head.

We need to prioritise juggling these roles, so that our different worlds do not hurt each other.

CONTENT VS PROCESS

We are going to go old school here. When we interact with someone, we can be aware of the conversation on one or two levels. The obvious level is the topic discussed, the words spoken, the opinions shared. This is what you would take away if a transcript was prepared after your talk together. This is called **content**. It is important, but it is only the tip of the iceberg.

Under this obvious level, what is happening beneath the surface? This is the *'why'* of the conversation; it is about seeking to understand the person's background, agenda, loaded issues, fears and personal vulnerabilities. This is called observing the **process level**, and it is where the main substance of the conversation truly lies. If you want to engage well with someone, you need to be clued into their process. You need to look for all of the extra information you can learn, from the extra bits they say to their non-verbals and background factors at play. This is about seeking to understand the *meaning* behind their words and actions. This is about having truly skilled communication and really understanding the why.

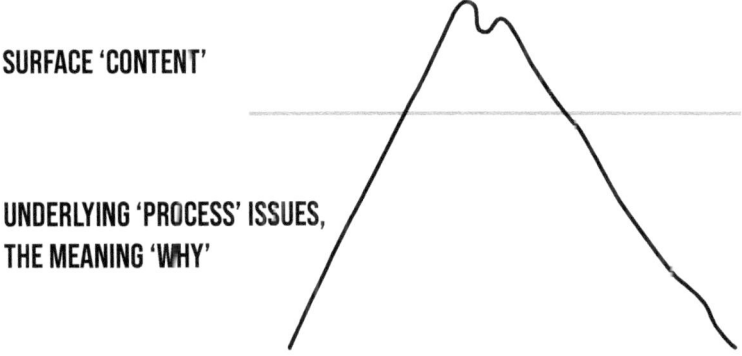

SURFACE 'CONTENT'

UNDERLYING 'PROCESS' ISSUES, THE MEANING 'WHY'

An example is a wife who wants her husband to do a particular task for her parents. She insists, while he refuses, saying he's busy and it shouldn't be up to him to do it anyway. He says the wife's brother should do it. The argument continues just on this superficial content level and they go around and around in circles. The 'whys' of the conversation, the underlying meaning and reason for their perspectives, is a completely different story. The husband feels that since they have been having marital problems his wife has been complaining to her parents about him. He feels that they are now going to be negative towards him. He feels on the outside. He feels hurt and angry at them (abandoned after many good years in the family), and fears seeing them. The wife's perspective is that she is trying to bridge the relationship between her husband and her parents, given they are trying to repair their relationship as a couple. If he does this task, she hopes it will help her parents' opinion of him. If he doesn't, she fears the tension will get worse. She feels extra pressure as she has already put him forward to do the task. She is angry at herself. She is fretting and scared. They are both heated in their reactivity, but neither is actually explaining or talking about their true motivations. If they spoke on this raw and honest causal level, they could have compassion for each other. They could work it through and support each other.

The ability to do this is a true gem of interpersonal skill and wisdom. If you can learn to function on this in-depth level you will become extremely efficient and effective in resolving your conflict issues.

HEARING WITHOUT LISTENING

One of the most fundamental of our communication skills is the art of mindful listening. We are often pretty ordinary with our listening skills. We're half-hearted and lacking in attentiveness, and only let part of the information seep through. When we don't listen – *really* listen – this leads to inevitable disconnection, because communication is the sharing of information. If that information is not received then we can feel unimportant, frustrated and hurt.

We all want to be heard, so we need to get much better at listening. It is only then that we can feel understood. Hearing without listening: this concept is very true, and it's a real problem. *Hearing* is simply the awareness of noise vibrations. We may even be able to repeat back the words without being deliberate or thoughtful in our attention. *Listening* is being active; we are intentionally and thoughtfully decoding what a person is saying in their verbal and non-verbal language. Listening involves prioritising the other person, and it is validation that while we may not agree, we are working to understand them.

> *Silence is one of our great arts of conversation.*
> Cicero, Roman philosopher

PARAPHRASING

When we are talking about important issues, either deeply personal or areas of tension perhaps, a vital step to active listening is showing that we *understand* what the other person is saying. We use verbal affirming comments and open body language to show that we are engaged. **Paraphrasing** what they have just said really demonstrates that we have worked to understand them. We will not be perfect; we won't understand them completely, but we can demonstrate what we do understand, and then they can clarify the areas where we are off track in our understanding.

Paraphrasing is using our own words to briefly summarise what we think they have just said. 'So I understand that you feel it is not reasonable for me to ...', or, 'So you're saying that you're only really missing your dad now that time has gone by?' It is only after we have shown our understanding with paraphrasing and checked to see if there is more that they would like to add, that we can move to contribute our thoughts on the topic.

BAD TIME TO TALK

To actively listen we need to be able to concentrate. Internal factors like extreme fatigue, a headache, or a racing, stressed mind are legitimate obstacles. External factors like technology within sight or hearing, kids requiring attention, deafness or poor phone reception are also valid problems. Communication is important, so we should be selective and create a quality chunk of time to talk. We definitely need to avoid having in-depth conversations when there are those internal and external distractions. Put aside distractions if you can, or reschedule the conversation to a more quality time.

MY REBUTTAL

Many of us regularly half-listen to 'our person' while in fact we are preparing our rebuttal. We are far more concerned with what we contribute than what we are receiving from our person. Instead of active listening, we are rehearsing, rehashing, preparing for when it is our turn. This really means that we are talking to ourselves, as we are not taking the other person's input on board with any sincerity. Starting with a paraphrase is a great way to break this rebuttal habit, as it will help us continue to focus on their input until it is genuinely our turn to contribute our thoughts.

OBSERVE WHAT?

You can practise active listening and practise flexing this interpersonal muscle group by sincerely asking a loved one how they're going, what's been happening in their world lately, what's interesting, have they experienced any challenges? Your sincerity is demonstrated when you listen deeply to their response. How was their reaction to your question to begin with? Did they look comfortable with having this kind of intimate conversation right now? Did they answer immediately, or were they avoidant or wary about disclosing how they were going? Were they uncomfortable receiving the attention and being the focus of the conversation? Did they try to quickly turn the conversation away by asking the same of you? Watch their body language; do they look open or closed off? Have you timed the conversation well – do they look enthusiastic or are they distracted or not in the mood for this conversation?

These are all of your observations through your active listening before they have even begun to answer. Another way to practise active listening is not to interrupt when someone is speaking to you. Pay attention until the other person is completely finished speaking. When the person has finished speaking, take a breath before you respond.

Can you see the extraordinary wealth of information that we miss when we hear but don't listen, when we have our eyes and ears closed to their meaning? We all love to be heard and understood. Active listening allows us to become experts on each other, through our attention and our prioritising of each other. With our daily conversations we should be experts on each other's daily experiences, our perspectives on issues and our life involvements.

I see you.

TAKE IN SO MUCH MORE

One profound benefit to active listening is that this genuine intent allows us to learn about another's struggles – their pain and suffering. When people feel listened to, they feel connected to us; their guard is down, and they may choose to open up more. We can then learn how their background and their current struggles shape their moment-to-moment experiences. It is when we create this safe space that, as the listener, we also open up to take in so much more of what the other person is saying. Our attention is on them, not on what is in our heads.

Listen with curiosity. Then you will not only have informed compassion and empathy for them, but you will also see them on a three-dimensional level, with the depth of understanding that can only be achieved through active listening. Any gaps in your understanding can then fuel meaningful questions that you can ask. When they feel heard, there is attunement between you, and you can help to soothe their resistance and any insecure or fearful feelings. This of course furthers your connection even more. This is the skill set that is essential when someone is agitated and distressed. As those who act aggressively are usually acting out of fear and sadness, the skill of mindful listening allows their defences to drop and you can talk to the quietened person, not the threatened, angry person.

TALK LESS, LISTEN MORE

Mindful listening is truly an art, and cultivating it takes practice. With time, you'll get out of your own head and become more interested in the other person's experience. As with other mindfulness practices, notice when your mind begins to wander off, whether to thoughts in your own world or a rebuttal that you are formulating

Become aware that your attention has wandered off, then intentionally bring it back to the person across from you.

Be kind and patient with yourself. This is a skill to gradually refine and strengthen. As long as you are improving and it is your priority, then you're doing great. I think on our deathbed we will finally truly comprehend that we should have talked less and listened more. It is a life lesson that we seem to be blind to, or regularly forget as we relapse into our self-focused conversation. Let's learn this skill of active listening and benefit from it for the entirety of our lives instead.

THE ART OF COMPROMISE

First there was one, then there was two, and if you have kids, then you may have a whole tribe. When we are alone, we do not have to take others into account too much. When we enter a relationship, we all need to reorient our goals and adapt our approach to the small and big things in life. We need to take each other's needs, wants, schedules, families and constraints into account. We get lots of opportunities to practise the necessary art of compromise – whether to go out for dinner and when and where, whether to invite people along, and who? Particularly when we are miles apart in interests, it is an art to respect each other's perspectives and create windows so that each person's preferences can be met.

If we are not willing to adjust our approach to things – our routine, our priorities – and to take our partner or children into account, then we could be heading for a brick wall. If you have a single-person mindset, you are going to have conflict in the relationship, as your partner may feel that you are dictating and imposing your way onto them, or that you are not building a life together, but rather remaining a separate, single person in the relationship.

Compromise is the basic ingredient necessary for connectedness in relationships to evolve over time. It is actually extremely good for us personally to practise thinking about others and being mindful of their needs as well as our own. It can rescue us from becoming overly self-focused, from becoming rigid and restrictive in our life approach. It can also allow us one of life's greatest joys: that of giving to and nurturing others. It can broaden our world because there are now two people painting the canvas of our life, so the breadth of life experience can grow and expand between us. We are less likely to continue going around and around in our own safe circles.

COPYING OUR PARENTS?

Here is a human irony: we spend our teens and early twenties actively forging our own path, and often doing so with an attitude that says we're not following our parents' paths. Some people invest a lot of time creating who they are by being different from their parents. But then in our thirties we look back and see how much we do precisely what our parents do. This is not always the case, of course - many of us go our own path, or go the opposite way – but nevertheless, there is often a clear pattern of copying our parents in certain ways. The reason is that what we witnessed as children becomes a template for all our future relationships. This is like a model of relating, and it is largely subconscious.

We can break away from this mould of previous generations. To depart from our previous mould and make other choices, we need a great deal of self-awareness and determination. It takes courage to create a new way of relating to others. Often in our determination not to follow our parents' example we can actually go the opposite way and end up with the opposite traits. For example, someone who grew up with a volatile, angry parent might hate this in their lives and detest it in their parent, so they develop almost an allergy to anger; they consciously regulate any hint of anger they feel and calm it, deny its expression. They can become incredibly and mindfully calm as an adult. Again, this takes insight, determination and courage.

When we run into conflict in our current relationships, this often triggers our history, our memories and past wounds that stem from our dysfunctional childhood experiences. As a result, we can feel incredibly uncomfortable. We are likely to fall into old patterns of reactivity when we feel trapped or threatened. These are behavioural patterns that are thoroughly encoded through a lot of previous rehearsal over and over again throughout our childhood. The issue of our template of love was covered in Chapter 3 of this book. As children, we have fundamental needs for security and stability. When our parents are not able to tune into these needs, we learn to relate to others with this resulting insecurity.

Let's go back. If our earliest exposure to relationships was dysfunctional, then we run the risk of repeating this dysfunctional way of relating with our partner, children, family, friends and work colleagues. If we come from a high-conflict family, for example, where there is an aggressive approach between family members, we may learn to have this eruptive response when we are in disagreements. In contrast if we spent our childhood fearful of this conflict and hiding in the shadows, this avoidant behaviour is likely to continue. We may not know how to handle conflict, and in our passive style, we would do anything to avoid the uncomfortable emotions associated with it. If we have not had our needs heard and met in our early years, then as adults we may feel really uncomfortable voicing our needs or having them prioritised. We may almost routinely put others' needs before our own, apologise compulsively for no reason, and feel incapable of saying no.

The template that we adopt from our childhood really depends on the role that we played during this learning process. For example, if we grew up with conflict and we were a part of it, as adults we may find ourselves routinely creating conflict, seeking out the drama of it, or the power over others. We are not conscious of what we are doing; we are just doing what we have always done. This dysfunction is how we know to relate to others. The problem is that we continue this legacy of doing harm to others. If we behave aggressively, it continues the cycle of hurt. We become the cause of emotional pain, in the same way that our parents were to us. We can become the bully ourselves, demeaning others, abusing our position of power. We can find ourselves frequently in this downward cycle. Without insight and determination, we continue this damaging power dance. This is why it is essential to become self-aware and skilled in sorting out our hot issues and increasing our emotional regulation. These skills are of course the core to this book.

What is the communication culture in your family, the way that you speak with and treat each other? Is there support and constructive communication, or critical humour? Do people cut each other down for mistakes, look for weaknesses, bitch about each other, not actively listen, or talk over each other? Some families have extreme disconnection and are like ships in the night. When they are in the same room, they often do not interact, only speaking with the superficial 'How's your day?' 'Good'.

Another common problem is parents passing on their own insecurities and neuroses. I mentioned earlier the contagious effect that parent depression and anxiety can have on children. If we model a fearful or hopeless outlook about the world, our children will learn that outlook.

Another epidemic-sized problem being passed on through the value system of families is an overemphasis on looks and image. If we, as a child, learn from an adult that our value comes from our packaging, image, looks or perceived status, then we are learning a dangerous value system in which our core selves are not really valued. We are being set up to live with a continual fear of inadequacy and judgement from others. This is because a superficial value system gives the power for our confidence to *others* – it allows others to judge our worth. This superficial value system not only has no validity or substance, but it creates a dangerous pathway to a whole dimension of negative self-talk and, with it, chronic anxiety, depression and seriously damaged quality of life.

The question is: do you want to continue to subscribe to the communication style from your family culture? What do you want to keep and what do you want to throw away or grow out of? With this question comes a lot of personal reflection. Are your loved ones feeling better or worse from their relationship with you? Are they feeling heard and understood; are you an expert in understanding your family members' worlds? Are you being constructive or destructive in your approach to your relationships and yourself?

If you realise something is broken, this is the time to fix it. Absorb the knowledge and the wisdom that you have figured out about your humanness, and get active. Dive in and sort through your issues. Use the earlier chapters as a resource to get busy. I am wishing you the gift of recognising your habitual patterns that are unhealthy and creating the space to make change.

EMOTIONS AND LISTENING

Our emotional state, as a close cousin to our attribution style, shapes how we listen to others. If we are feeling happy, we are more likely to filter out negative behaviours from others, and we will notice and absorb more positive interactions around us. The reverse is also true: when we are feeling negative, anxious, depressed or stressed, we will be on the lookout for negative interactions and absorb this extra negativity. We hear more what is wrong with what is being said than what is right. We lose our generosity. We may not even notice positive interactions; we may ignore them or discount them.

It is so important to comprehend that the way we mould interpretation of interactions with others is based on *what we bring to the equation*. Our emotional baseline creates our experience to a huge degree. Rather than listening and calmly problem solving, when we are in a negative mood state we are primed to react to a perceived threat with the old fight, flight, faint, freeze model, which is usually not at all helpful. We need to at least realise that we are part of our own problem, to try to observe our vulnerable, negative emotional state and work on our ability to read the situation in a more neutral, objective way.

Being mindful allows us to notice these tricky reactions of ours. We can work to come back to the present and acknowledge our feelings. When we acknowledge and are gentle with our discomfort, we quieten ourselves down and become less reactive. We are being more reflective. We can move to self-compassion, which is the doorway to empathy, compassion, and connection with the other person. In this mode of self-compassion, it is great to actually say, 'I'm not in a great headspace right now, so we just need to tread water for a bit until I am back to myself again'. Or, 'I just need some space at the moment'. Or, 'This is really an important issue and I want to give it the energy it deserves; right now, however, I'm not up to it. Let's come back to this soon'. We own our mood state and the fact that we are a bit of a liability in that moment. We can work to minimise harm we may cause and explain that we need to reschedule our chat for a more productive time. It is vital of course that we *do* come back to the issues at hand. If we continue to avoid or ignore, we will create understandable frustration and distrust.

MANAGING INTIMIDATING BEHAVIOUR

Whether it be at home with our family, at work, with friends, or with acquaintances or strangers, there are countless occasions where we experience an interaction that is difficult to manage. It is hurtful, and we can quickly feel overwhelmed. It is horrible to be on this receiving end. One reason these difficult situations are so painful is that they trigger a deep fear that perhaps we all carry: a fear of not being accepted by others. We may feel rejected, judged, not seen, not acknowledged or supported. How do we still find the courage to engage with them? How do we manage these interactions?

When we come across these intimidating interactions, we typically respond in autopilot mode; we easily spin into a fight, flight, faint, freeze reaction. Our thoughts, emotions and sensations spiral and deteriorate. The stress builds and we respond with avoidance, or passive-aggressive behaviour, or feeling like a victim, or being aggressive and confrontational ourselves in return. Chances of addressing the issue, of being constructive and reconciling, are pretty much out the window.

While the passive response of ignoring and avoiding the intimidating behaviour provides temporary relief, it really just makes the situation worse. Frustration in the other person is likely to build, and they will feel confused and come back more flared up; then the situation can escalate. The option of submitting to a verbal attack and allowing the other person to get their way without standing up for yourself is not at all a good option. When you are being passive or behaving like a victim, over time your self-respect is chipped away. You feel like a doormat. This is not an okay role to play.

The strategy of being aggressive and fighting back is another poor option. In the short term, it can feel good;

you can feel like you get a sense of self-respect from fighting back. But fighting back completely undermines any ability to find mutual understanding. It creates a destructive dynamic. It can make us further lose our attuned connection and can do insurmountable damage to the person that we care about.

Let's learn the skills of responding to intimidating behaviour. This involves skilful deflection designed to protect yourself *and* the other person from being hurt more. The goal is to neutralise their aggressive behaviour and to take out the sting. It would be an extraordinary feat to actually transform the interaction into one of attunement and connection.

The first step is to actually *approach and engage* in the interaction. We enter into their intimidating conversation rather than avoid or submit. A way to feel confident in doing this is to remember that provided the person does not have a tricky personality disorder (see 'Tricky people', Chapter 21 of this book), then their aggression is actually an expression of their stress. They are not well within themselves if they are behaving in this way. It is almost guaranteed that underneath their hostility is vulnerability, fear or sadness that they are not managing well.

Try putting yourself in their shoes. This is a big ask when they are being intimidating towards you. But if you can ask yourself how you would feel in their situation, with their struggles, from the outside world or due to their current limitations, then you can be less intimidated by their behaviour. Instead you can see it as a mask, or as an acting out of their vulnerable underlying issues. It is important through this process to practise mindful listening. Use your tone of voice as well as your words to convey that you are listening. Listen to their words *and* the meaning and emotion behind their words. Ask about their beliefs and feelings about the situation, such as, 'Explain to me what is going on for you', or 'Help me understand what you are saying and why you are saying it'. This allows you to understand where they are coming from, as well as effectively triggering an empathetic approach from you. They will receive the message that you are approaching the situation with the goal of understanding, not winning or dominance.

The second step is to *find areas where you agree*. The goal is to foster alignment where it may be forged. Through your mindful listening, you have sought out any concerns, emotions or perspectives that you can also relate to. When you find themes that resonate with you, you can genuinely validate the other person's experiences. This needs to be authentic. Don't try to fake that you agree; most people will read through this façade. This approach is all about genuine attunement with the person who you originally found intimidating. Verbalise these areas where you relate; for example: 'Yes, I also struggle to find time to get everything done', or, 'If someone was that rude to me at work, I wouldn't enjoy working with them either'. Or, 'Yes, it can feel like we will never catch up with the bills'.

The third stage is about *leading and motivating* the interaction towards a more positive and co-operative approach. It is about building goodwill between you in order to work it through and come up with a solution. This is about improving morale and getting everyone on board for positive change. You could perhaps say, 'We are both having a rough time with this; what can we do to move out of this dark experience? What can we work to improve on?' We realise that we can be on the same team and can work together to find a way to improve the situation.

The fourth stage is about brainstorming ideas, through which we can *explore a compromise*, or respect each other's opinions, but not necessarily come to an agreement. Respectfully done, we can agree to disagree.

The fifth stage then involves exploring *mutually agreeable ideas*. You are working through your connection; you are working with a shared goal. What is a compromise that is mutually agreeable? This can be a plan in the short term, mid term or long term. The decision might be, now that you understand each other, that you are going to agree to disagree, but respectfully so. If you cannot come up with a solution, then be more creative, or work to accept it when things don't go your way. Perhaps go back and explore the problem again and find areas that you *do* agree on. We can and need to be up for review.

To be skilled in responding to intimidating behaviour, it is important to be mindful of your own mental and emotional state. This is the foundation for your ability to remain centred and to regulate your emotional response when faced with hostile behaviour. Notice how your body is reacting. Is your body stiff or tense? It is understandable to respond with this discomfort. See these body cues as information. Be aware of your thoughts and feelings, and your immediate response of wanting to avoid or escape the other person's unpleasant behaviour. This is a cue to relax your muscles, focus on your breath, and self-talk your way to being as calm and rational as possible. When you do this, you are in the present; you are centring yourself and creating the space to respond mindfully. You can respond in a proactive – not reactive – way, with more reflection, creativity and flexibility.

Now keep in mind, this is a tough thing to do. This will require a lot of patience and compassion as you negotiate this challenging interaction. Be kind to yourself and acknowledge this as legitimately difficult communication. Be your own cheer squad or coach. Encourage yourself that you'll get through this, and that your stress response is understandable. As with all things worth doing, it will take time and practice to develop this skill of working through intimidating behaviour. It is okay to respond initially with fear and anger; this is an understandable and even intelligent response to intimidating behaviour. The key is to identify and ground your automatic response rather than to dive in and continue to react to it.

There are a few more exceptions to look out for. If the person is triggering your hot issues, for example, it may not feel safe to engage. Or if it becomes clear that they are determined to have conflict. In that case, they do not want to find a resolution; they do not want to have a breakthrough together. Perhaps they are a tricky person (Chapter 21) after all? Or perhaps you cannot agree on what the problem is, or your beliefs and approaches to the issue are just diametrically opposed? When we are fundamentally on different pages, we can agree to disagree, but we can still manage the process of empathising with their distress, even when we believe it is ignorantly held.

Of course, if there is ever a risk of danger or harm, psychologically or physically, do not engage. Do not put yourself in the firing line and endanger or martyr yourself. Another reality is that sometimes it is best to take half an hour out and just calm the emotion down so that your analytical brain is more available. But make sure that you reengage in a timely way; otherwise you are avoiding for the sake of avoidance. It is a skill to know when to engage and when to allow some breathing room first; this is healthy relationship wisdom. The ability to defuse emotionally charged situations relies on attunement, empathy and mindfulness. It is a skill that sets you up to feel more confident with interpersonal challenges that will cross your path all through your life.

Perhaps the greatest gift and the key to ensuring our relationships are healthy is our ability to listen deeply.

To listen with emotional resonance, genuine interest and care. This mindfulness practice leads us to have compassion for our loved ones, and strangely also to have self-compassion. It is a dance and we need to be aware of ourselves as much as the other person. We all have a deep yearning to be heard and understood, to be seen for who we really are. Being heard and understood is perhaps the purest experience of love. Practising mindfulness, self-compassion, and loving kindness will be very helpful. Perhaps the greatest key to friendship and connection lies in the ability to listen deeply, with interest, care, and emotional resonance. Many of us have a deep yearning to be heard, and often one of the greatest gifts we can offer to others is to listen.

CHAPTER 9
WHAT IS YOUR CAPACITY FOR PERSPECTIVE TAKING?

How good are you at **perspective taking**? This is about putting yourself into the other person's experience and imagining how they might think and feel. If you were to freeze a conversation, could you put yourself into the other person's mind and work out what they are thinking about the issue or situation? What is their perspective? What is their experience and their emotional response? Take it another layer: why are they thinking and feeling that way? What is the relevant background that is shaping them right now? Perspective taking is your ability to gather information about the other person. You cannot work through an issue unless you can recognise and see the other person's point of view.

Reading each other.

The question of your ability to *understand the other person's perspective* is separate to whether you are *open to their opinions*. This is about whether you can understand what their opinion is in the first place. This is about the mechanics. Some people are extremely skilled at perspective taking and, on the dark side, some people use those skills to manipulate others. On the positive side, it is a skill that enables us to be able to work effectively alongside each other because we have more information to work with. Some people are naturally skilled here, while many need to improve their people skills through learning to understand how other people view and experience things.

If you struggle and feel a bit clueless about what other people are thinking and feeling, you can learn this skill described below.

Slow it down, take a moment. Stop and contemplate, and based on the information you have, ask yourself what the other person could be thinking or feeling. Try these tips:

- Listen closely to what they are saying, rather than focusing on your own argument or rebuttal.

- Ask yourself: why might they be saying what they are saying?

- What are the background conversations on this topic – what has he said previously?

- What is her facial expression: positive or negative? If negative, can you pin it down? Is it sadness, fear, frustration, desperation?

- What is his body telling you? Is he cowering away, looking for an exit? Is he looking fearful? Is he antsy, moving around, fingers, hands or limbs jittering; is he anxious or agitated? Is he standing, trying to make himself look big or confident, arms out, shoulders out, perhaps hands behind his head? Is he trying to intimidate, or look more confident then he actually feels? Body language is the mother lode of information ... it's all there; we just have to look.

- Take note of his tone of voice. What emotion can you hear? Is it a begging tone (which hints at desperation), or an apprehensive tone (suggesting fear or a feeling of intimidation), or an angry tone, or is it a positive, constructive tone?

- Here is a big one: to be able to comprehend another person's perspective, try putting aside *your* perspective for a moment. This can be really hard if we ourselves are being triggered. So the question to ask yourself is, 'Am I reacting, am I being triggered?' We have to recognise if this is happening first, so that we can park it sideways for a moment and open our brains to understand the other person's perspectives. Are you taking your problems, your issues, out on the other person? An example is a thirty-year-old female who I am working with at the moment. She has come from a highly, highly critical, domestically violent relationship and she is now with a loving, healthy partner. When her new partner says that he is having difficulties with something in his life, my client immediately launches into a defensive belief that this is a criticism of her. My client cannot park her fear of being criticised long enough to hear her new partner's perspective. Indeed, it's actually got nothing to do with her. These are her 'hot issues'.

I have worked with children and teenagers who have struggled with perspective taking. We would watch a favourite TV show of theirs and, much to their annoyance, I would pause the show and ask them to explain to me what the different characters' perspectives were. This was a safe start to improving perspective-taking skills because the client was not personally involved. They would not do so well at the start, but as I prompted them to look for surrounding information to work out the characters' perspectives, they gradually and impressively improved. It was like being an investigator and looking for clues. We would then graduate to real-world interactions, which was harder because they had to pause their own perspective and their emotion to tap into reading the other person's perspective.

We as adults can continue to refine our perspective-taking skills throughout our life. Perhaps the hardest part is parking our perspective and our emotional reactions to take a moment to understand what the other person is thinking and feeling.

CHAPTER 10
THE FEMALE WANTS TO FEEL HEARD, AND THE MALE WANTS TO GO STRAIGHT TO THE FIX

If there was any comic strip between the sexes, this story I'm about to tell you would have to be it. I need to warn you, this contains some generalised statements across the sexes. Of course there are many exceptions to this pattern, and I celebrate the broad sweep of individuals out there. I am purely talking about gender *trends* more generally, not gender absolutes. I am also refering to the dynamic between males and females. I joke with clients that males and females are not compatible. While I jest, I do see some clear advantages in same-sex relationships when it comes to this topic. Let me explain.

We really are ridiculous in the degree that males and females can and do routinely get this wrong. So here we go ... The female *usually* primarily wants to feel heard and understood. She wants the glorious relief of her partner knowing what's on her mind. She speaks to her partner, usually in paragraphs. She wants them to demonstrate to her that they have comprehended what she is saying. She doesn't need them to fix things; she just needs them to understand.

If the partner is male, then he *usually* listens, decides what he thinks is the issue and then – in his lovely desire to help and be of use to her – he responds with a solution, 'a fix-it'. She does not want him to fix it at this stage, however; this is too early in her processing. She wants him to let her know that he understands how she feels and how she sees the problem. When he does not communicate this understanding, she may repeat, and repeat, trying to get him to understand her. If the woman is in a same-sex relationship, then perhaps her female partner will match her in staying at the 'talking through' stage.

The male, however, is *usually* sitting there thinking, *What does she want me to do? I've tried to fix it, but she's not responding to my suggestions; she just keeps repeating the problem, over and over again. And she is getting more upset?* He is feeling inadequate, a failure, and impotent. He might try one more time to give his helpful fix-it solution. She cuts him down and just gets increasingly annoyed with him. Somehow the problem has become about *him*. He is very confused. He thinks, *Okay, this is bad, I'm going to withdraw because this is not working and I'm getting really annoyed.* He's irritated, even angry. He is taking responsibility for his anger and withdrawing to calm himself down. Well done!

She sees this and gets more upset, however. She feels that he is withdrawing because he does not care about her in that moment; he really doesn't care to understand her feelings and problems. With this, he withdraws further into his cave (shed, bedroom, garage, anywhere!). She pursues, still talking, and begging for him to hear her. He feels trapped, his desperation peaks into anger. He erupts with some sort of anger outburst, which is saying 'Get back'. She is shocked, hurt and confused. She decides that he has an anger problem. She is not aware that she has accidentally antagonised him, because she has been so consumed by her own emotional desperation.

> She wants him to paraphrase his understanding of her experience, not to fix her problem.

This may not be you. Or this may be you on a regular basis, but in any case it is a common, disastrous dance between the genders. What to do? He needs to learn not to think that it is his role to fix the female's problems, or at least to understand that she does not want this *in the first instance*. She wants him to use words to paraphrase his understanding and empathy for her. She could help him. She could simply say, 'I don't want you to fix this; I want you to listen and then let me know what you have heard me say.' She can even guide him further; she can ask him to paraphrase ('What do you think I am trying to say?'). Before you know it they will be speaking the same language, not getting lost in misunderstandings.

CHAPTER 11
EXPERIENCE SEX, DON'T DO SEX

This section contains a long shopping list of some of the sex-related issues that we often work through in psychology sessions. Sex comes up in session all the time when clients brainstorm their top stressors. Sex is a topic that they are relieved to finally untangle. Getting some direction in this area often brings comfort. The following topics are areas of misinformation and bundles of hurdles that trip us up in the bedroom. Some you may relate to, and some you might not. While the gender generalisations might not apply to you, I hope this section will help you explore what you *do* relate to and what does makes sense for you to take on board.

There are basically three big hurdles to sex: getting distracted in life, different gender views of when and why to have sex, and how we relate to sex as an individual and as a couple. Again, it's an ambitious topic, but even a crash course in this topic is a positive launch forward.

The root cause of the broad range of sexual problems is usually in our heads. We can get so stressed about sex that we forget to enjoy it. Some people are going through a checklist of things that they have to do during sex. They are thinking too much, in a pressure state. They are not in the state of savouring, exploration and creativity. He may be thinking *Don't lose my erection, don't finish too quick*. She may be thinking *Can I orgasm*? and this may create tension and space between them. We can be too busy *doing* sex, rather than *experiencing* sex. We can think that sex is about orgasm. With sex, we need to get out of our heads and into our bodies. When we let go of thinking about the outcome, we can connect with our sexual sensations and enjoy that very moment for what it is.

Sex is about self-love, intimacy and connection.

PLAN TO HAVE A GREAT SEX LIFE

Life is busy and life consumes us with distractions. Sex can easily become lost from our focus in our busy day, week and month. In our society where we are all on our phones and screens, we can become disconnected, and this lack of connection with the moment can get in the way with sex.

But how wonderful is great sex? Sex gives us time for play. We can give pleasure to our partner, we bond in our intimacy, and we can feel a beautiful sense of contentment in being a lovely lover. Sex is even good for our health. Research has found that orgasms are linked to reducing stress, enhancing sleep, boosting hormone levels and curbing appetite. Yet we get distracted and sex falls from our focus as a couple. You can *decide* to be a great lover. What a lovely ambition and art form to continue to refine. To be a great lover, however, is less about *doing*, and more about *understanding*. It is not about you; it is about your partner.

> Sex is supposed to be fun and playful.

The loveliest chocolate, wine, massage or scenic view will all become normal to us and even boring if we experience it continually and in the same way. Sex is the same. Like other pleasures, unless we keep sex fresh, we habituate. It loses its spark. We are always learning; we need to keep discovering new possibilities in our partner and ourselves. This is a dance that continues for life. Sex is about our consciousness, our response, and we will never reach the end of this landscape. Through knowing our partner and learning to share ourselves, we can have joint adventures in our sex lives. This is about embracing and steering our sexuality and cultivating this aspect of ourselves as we continue to explore our complexity. Most importantly, don't get lost down the rabbit hole of life. Don't get distracted by life and forget the beautiful dimension of your sexuality.

YOUR TURN

Both partners need to initiate sex; there needs to be balance here. If you have noticed in your relationship that one of you initiates sexual intimacy and the other does not, then stop and talk about it. You have a problem.

This is even more the case if the sexual advances are regularly being shut down and rejected by one partner. What is happening for the partner who doesn't want the intimacy? What are the problems in the relationship or their issues on a personal level? The initiating partner is going to be feeling rejected because their approaches are not being reciprocated or because they are being shut down. They are probably not feeling desired because they themselves are not being approached by their partner for sex.

It is crucial to talk warmly and constructively about these issues and, more importantly, to listen deeply to each other. It is only when you talk and listen that you can solve this problem, so that you can move forward and be more on the same page together. It is not an option to just shut sex out of your relationship. This avoidance will inevitably lead to distancing, becoming more like roommates, and a building sense of hurt and rejection. Get healthy if you want a healthy future together.

YOUR LIBIDO

From talking to thousands of men and women in session about their libido experiences, I would have to be blind not to observe clear patterns of gender difference. *Broadly* and *generally* speaking, men report that after having sex their libido subsides, and their libido engine takes a momentary break. Within that day their engine starts to turn over again. Their libido engine is idling most of the time; they are usually *perhaps* 2/10 in the mood for sex. It is in the background, and unless there is a clear stressor going on, they can fairly readily think sex is a good idea. The more they connect with it, think about it and get stimulated by their environment, and the more time that passes without sex, the more intense their sexual contemplation and building of sexual energy. This is not pleasant; this is often a gnawing feeling and a distraction. If they are, however, throughly distracted or stressed by life, then they often describe not experiencing this building up of sexual pressure.

As for women: again, *generally speaking*, thousands have shared with me that their libido engine ignition only really gets started if a priming situation comes along. Even when the sex is great and tailored to them, women can go through their days with their libido at 0/10. Sex is not in their usual framework. Actually, many women tell me that they can go for six months without any thought of sex.

The libido engine typically starts for the females when there is a romantic connection happening, when there is a visual stimulus, when she is enjoying flirtation, when she is really feeling connected with her partner, when she feels they are powering along well together, or they are in bed with gentle caressing turning their attention to her sensuality. If they are stressed or tired, or there is relationship frustration, disconnection or conflict, sex is often the opposite to what women want to do. Sex at this time makes no sense, as sex is the cherry on top of a good moment or connection.

Of course the quality of the sex and the woman's capability to relax and connect with her sensual self is another major factor in whether she has a positive attitude towards sex in the first place. But day in, day out, unless the key turns in the engine, her libido engine is off. If the male can induce her, her engine starts, but often she just reports that she is not in the mood. Which is true. So, what to do?

So are men and women compatible in the bedroom? Well, in heterosexual relationships you could argue that the answer is no, not really, if you think about how we seem to be programmed. The guys are quick to have their 'on duty' sign up, and the girls don't even reach for their sign unless there is a good reason. This is a problem. Men and women need to get into each other's heads and experiences to understand each other and find a middle ground. No one is right; we are just different. Same-sex relationships *may* have some significant advantages here, since they are relationships between two people who perhaps have similar patterns with their libido.

The female really needs to learn that she cannot wait until her libido is purring along, because she has to start the engine first. She needs to learn that if she puts herself into the situation, then her libido will start to warm up. As noted earlier, it is crucial that both partners initiate sex (semi-regularly) so that they both feel desired. The key is for a woman to find a time that works for her and to initiate sex with her partner, not because she is in the mood, but because she knows that she will get in the mood. She has to learn not to wait for herself, but to make it happen. In heterosexual relationships, the male needs to get into the female's head and realise that she needs to be primed by a connected relationship to want sex. It is the health of her headspace and their relationship that puts her in the mood for sex. The male has to focus on these foundation issues, not only because this will prime her for sex, but also because, hopefully, he wants to develop this healthy standard in their relationship.

There are so many wins with this approach; it provides a helping hand that many heterosexual relationships need. She can initiate sex at a time that works better for her; he feels desired; she gets a happier partner; she gets to connect with her sexuality; they both enjoy the sensual pleasures and they connect as a couple.

SEX, WHEN?

I'm going to make some more gender statements here. These are generalisations that apply to perhaps most of us, and complicate relationships for people in heterosexual relationships. It's interesting to consider what you can relate to here and to reflect on your personal patterns. *In general*, as discussed in the previous section, males often experience connectedness through sex. They can see sex as an ingredient for getting on track as a couple; sex lines the stars up for them. For women, on the other hand, sex comes as a response to the stars already being lined up, when they feel the relationship is already in a positive state.

If the woman is really disconnected in the relationship, then she is not likely to want sex. She may think that she has a low libido, when in truth her libido is hibernating because she is unhappy. In hetero relationships, the clincher is that the male is often far more engaged and attentive in his relationship if he is having regular sex. But it is this contented, more attentive male that the woman wants, who will inspire her to want sex. So which comes first? The more attentive male, or sex? A quandary. We are typically not compatible as men and women when it comes to this dance of sex.

This is extremely tricky because the woman should not have sex unless it is what she absolutely wants to do. She should never be pressured to have sex, nor agree to this pressure. But when there is an active sex life, as well as the connection and bonding that it generates, the male can feel more connected and switched on to the female. So perhaps a middle ground is the answer. The male works to be more mindful of her needs and perhaps her stressors pre-sex (in a supportive, not a fix-it role), and the female does not wait until all the stars are completely aligned and all is well with their relationship before having sex. She might be a bit generous because then she gets the more attentive husband that she craves.

It is a common problem for men and women to have little understanding of each other's sexual needs and patterns. The men relate from their perspective, thinking women should think like them and be always ready for sex. While women assume that the men should share their perspective and their approach to sex as an intimate expression of a healthy relationship.

Men can find woman incomprehensible and in general they are able to acknowledge it. In contrast, I have found that women *think* they understand the men in their lives, and are shocked when they find out they actually don't have much of a clue. Sex is one of the areas of confusion we can put on the table and clear up. It doesn't mean that we come any closer to being on the same page, but at least we can learn what page we are both reading from.

THAT'S NOT SEX

What *is* sex? Is it intercourse? Let's break it down. Let's get anatomical. Why? Because quite frankly I spend a lot of time talking about these issues, and we need the basics nice and clear so we can build from there. Many clients are self-conscious about their limited knowledge in this area. If only they knew how common this gap in knowledge was.

So let's go. For men, orgasm-triggering nerves are mostly on the head of the penis. Intercourse stimulates these nerves in a big way, making intercourse for most men lead to orgasm. For women, most orgasm-triggering nerves are *not* located within the vagina, but in the clitoris, the small bundle of nerve tissue that sits just above the vaginal opening, in the vulva (which I will explain below). The clitoris is just inside the vulva lips. It is the sensual stimulation of the clitoris that creates orgasm for women. Intercourse itself does not focus on the clitoris, however; it focuses on the internal part of the female anatomy, the vagina. Yep! The part without the limited amount of orgasm-inducing nerve endings. Here lies the problem with intercourse.

So how does a woman orgasm with intercourse? Well, put crudely, intercourse it seems is designed more for the male anatomy than female. And yet we routinely think that intercourse equates to sex. We have a problem in logistics, as 60-75% of women do *not* experience enough stimulation on their clitoris during intercourse to reach orgasm. For most women, intercourse literally misses the target.

So again, what is sex if it is not the historical concept of intercourse equals orgasm – for both men and women?

If you break it down, it seems we are physically designed for sex to be first clitoral play until the woman orgasms, and then intercourse to allow the man to orgasm and perhaps for the woman to greedily have a second orgasm. Women are designed so that if they have intercourse after orgasming through clitoral play, then they may be able to orgasm again (and again!). This is one of the strengths of the female anatomy. Unlike men, they can come back for more in a crescendo kind of way. Intercourse, to its credit, plays a special role as it can create that closeness in experiencing such intimacy together.

So, if we are having traditional sex that is just intercourse, intercourse, intercourse, then the female – who, statistically, is unlikely to experience orgasm through intercourse – will find that sex is not working for her. And if it is not working for her, then in the longer term, why would she want to have sex with her partner? If you're doing something and it's not working for you, you stop. This quickly becomes another very important factor that can dampen the female's likelihood of reaching out or taking up the suggestion of sex from the man.

Perhaps during the honeymoon period, the woman was so full of an avalanche of brain chemicals that she wanted passionate sex all the time. When they then move through this stage, the couple might find that she is just not interested in sex because it is not working for her. So many men have said to me that their wife is not the sexual creature that they married. Meanwhile they have had no discussion about why. They remain ignorant to each other's world, and their sexual problems spiral and get ever more complicated.

MIND OVER SEX

Then there is our consciousness, our mind. Once we have worked out our physical anatomy, we work out pretty quickly how enjoyable sex is based on our headspace. We can experience the same sex act as ecstatic, pleasurable and enjoyable, or unpleasant, revolting and even painful, depending on how we are feeling and relating to the action and our partner. The mood between us as a couple guides our playfulness and our capacity to connect with sensations and be playful. This is about our mind, not our body.

SEXUAL KRYPTONITE

There is also the issue of pressure. Pressure is the kryptonite of good sex. Pressure from our partner to have sex or about how to have sex will make us shut down sexually. Pressure within ourselves means we will also absolutely shut down.

Good sex is playfulness; it is openness to ourselves and to our partners. With regard to sex, our confidence – our self-esteem – is a major player. It is the commentator that has us on board and positive or booing from the sideline causing conniptions of distress. It is important to talk to yourself in a positive, healthy way. Our body image comes into play here also – and how many of us are relaxed and positive about our bodies? Sadly, this is not the norm.

OUR DELECTABLE BODIES

If we feel ashamed of our body, then we are not going to allow exploration of it. Many feel disassociated from their bodies. Shame is the killer of sexuality. And this is not about physically looking any particular way; this is our headspace, how we *feel* about our bodies.

I know plenty of beautiful, shapely men and woman who feel comfortable and confident in their bodies, and plenty of catwalk men and woman who cannot stand their bodies. Body confidence is about our self-love and sense of safety with our partner; it is not actually about our physical bodies. Just as your fingerprint is unique, so too is your sexual anatomy. Penises and vulvas are unique to the individual, so just get on board; it is ridiculous to compare or worry about yours. There is no normal. There is just everyone being different. Is there a 'normal' fingerprint? No! Precisely my point. Just embrace yourself.

We don't have to earn our positive body image.

ASSERT YOUR DESIRES

Part of sexual confidence is being comfortable enough to ask for things in the bedroom – to speak up and let our partners know what is and is not working (in a positive way!). It is no surprise that research has found that as education and age increases, so does women's rates of orgasm. Why? Because better-educated women and older women are more likely to speak up and ask for what they want. They are more likely, for example, to ask for direct clitoral touch before intercourse. As women move away from the oppressive historical role of the submissive female (both in and out of the bedroom), they are more likely to be aware of and assert their own sexual needs and desires. They are more likely to explore and refine what works for their unique bodies.

We need to communicate our needs. It is a skill to feel relaxed to receive oral sex, for example. To be able to receive this attention and affection from our partners. This is a noble skill to refine. Sounds strange, but hey, this is truly embracing our femaleness. If women do not feel comfortable exploring their own sensuality, how can their male partners possibly work it out?

Women, you deserve pleasure.

THE CLITORIS MYSTERY

The female sexual organs are little understood by men and women. A woman can feel uncomfortable with her sexual body; she can feel self-conscious and even a sense of shame. There are limits to what her male lover can learn about her sexual needs if she is not confident to take the lead with her own body.

The clitoris is an interesting creature. But first things first. Many people say 'vagina' when they really mean 'vulva'. This is an extremely common misunderstanding, which just shows how undereducated we are about female sexuality and anatomy. So that women have personal authority over their bodies, we need to get this right. Imagine if we kept calling the penis a seminal vesicle? Weird, right? It is also crucial that we get this terminology right because every time we use the word 'vagina' when we really mean 'vulva', we are skipping the part that gives women the most pleasure. While the vagina is the part that usually gives heterosexual men the most pleasure, it is the vulva, the area of clitoral stimulation, that is the most important area for women in achieving orgasm.

So here are the facts: the **vulva** is the external organ that includes the clitoris and the labial lips, and the **vagina** is the internal muscular canal that connects the vulva to the uterus. The vagina is where babies pass through during childbirth, and it's the passage of a woman's menstrual flow and where the **G-spot** is located. While we are at it, the G-spot, or Gräfenberg spot, is located on the belly-button side of the vagina, a few inches inside the vagina. It swells when the woman is turned on – and yes, some women like the feeling of their G-spot being touched.

The internal clitoral system within the vulva is extraordinary and very complex. The structure of the clitoris was only mapped out by Dr Helen O'Connell in 1998. At the top is the clitoral gland, and coming down from it in the shape of a wishbone to either side is a pair of clitoral legs and a pair of clitoral bulbs. The clitoris has as much erectile tissue as the penis. It is as if women have internal erections. The clitoral gland has 8000 nerve endings, which is more than the penis has. The clitoris increases in sensitivity when touched very gently, and can easily become desensitised and even painful if touched roughly. But as the woman gets closer to orgasm, what she wants changes from the softness of butterfly kisses to gradually more pressure. The longer the woman can stretch out and build up her orgasm, the bigger and more powerful it will be.

How intricate is this dance? This is why it is essential that women know what they want and what works for them and why they need to steer their partner. It is the female's responsibility to choreograph the clitoral dance and to communicate clearly to her partner. With sex generally, both partners need to communicate and be open about what they prefer. Sex should never be a guessing game; this creates distance between partners in the bedroom.

VARIETY

Great sex means variety. While sometimes a couple may have intense sex from the beginning, it is also important to change it up and spend time to slowly build up arousal. This emotional intimacy is the **tantric** type, which means we build up and heighten sexual sensitivity and arousal, prolonging the arousal. Exploring sexual arousal involves harnessing our ability to concentrate in the moment. Here is a mindfulness exercise to practise! This is about learning to relax and receive, as well as listening to our partner in the art of sexually giving.

It takes time for most women to orgasm, with women often taking at least twenty minutes of sexual activity to climax. Orgasms become easier as we become more confident in the bedroom. It is important that women do not feel pressure to orgasm, as this in itself can get in the way of an orgasm. Think of it as taking a stroll, and enjoy it all along the way. Where you end up is a separate issue, and not of absolute importance. We need to embrace our sensual selves. Try not to limit yourself; exploration is a wonderful thing.

SEXUAL TRAUMA

Sexual trauma can create a barrier to sexual playfulness, which is then a barrier to sexual pleasure and enthusiasm. It really takes time, a working towards having a healthy head and positive alternative experiences to work through and defuse the pain of sexual trauma. The good news is with good therapy, support from loved ones and time, we can heal. The human capacity to heal is an extraordinary thing. We are a bit like starfish: different parts of us can grow back, and we can learn to feel safe and sexually playful again.

GOING SOLO

Masturbation is a great way to learn what you like, or to learn about using sex toys, either with your partner or solo. When we go solo, we can increase our connection with our sensuality, and we can then share this with our partner. Most of us – men and women – experienced our first orgasm through masturbation. This is how we learnt what we like.

Before vibrators were available to create clitoral stimulation, woman were very stuck with being able to reliably reach orgasm solo. These battery-operated helpers have allowed a dramatic growth in female sexual awakening and empowerment. It is wonderful now that women can buy clitoral vibrators online; they don't need to walk into a sex shop, something that many find an absolute deterrent. Women can now learn what they like. Historically, sex toys were shaped like penises. We now know that it is actually mostly the clitoris that needs the stimulation, so there is now the popular option of the discreet and small sex toys that are designed purely for clitoral stimulation.

They're just big enough to house small batteries. I have found their small, intimate size is less off-putting for both women and men. Many female clients are just wanting to learn gently and discreetly to become more sexually open. These small sex toys will also not make men feel as if they are a replacement for their penis, which they are not. Different tool, different job!

PORN EDUCATION

An absolute joke is how the female orgasm is depicted in pornography. It generally portrays an unrealistic image of the female routinely reaching orgasm through intercourse, like a man. Women are usually more complex then this in what they need to reach orgasm. This is tragic, as many youths are receiving their sex education and their sexual exposure through this porn fiction. This is like kids believing in cartoons. We really need to step away from porn, to step into the real world of people, where we learn through sensual touch and communication.

CREATIVE WITH TIME

Life is hectic. When can we possibly find time for sex? Well, part of a lovely sex life is creativity. So get creative.

I find it amusing when people with one child tell me they cannot find time for sex, then they look quizzically at me and say, 'You have five kids, right?' I'm not going to talk about my sex life in session, but I just smile back and say, 'Get creative, prioritise, don't allow excuses.'

Yes, we are fatigued and yes, we can feel that life is go, go, go. So look for the window when you are less fatigued – or better still, create these windows. When you are determined and it is a priority, you will reshuffle your other distractions. You can make it a precious, recharging, connecting time that works for you.

HOW DO YOU (MIS)INTERPRET INTIMATE ADVANCES?

What happens when the man approaches the woman for sex, and the female continues be uninterested? While this can happen with both genders, and across all sexual orientations, I have clinically seen this gender pattern much too often in heterosexual relationships. Over time she feels pressure from him because she knows he is feeling increasingly frustrated from her rejections. She becomes hypervigilant and interprets all of his approaches of daily affection as suggestions and pressure for sex. She shuts down these intimate advances because she doesn't want to encourage him, and she wants to avoid the conflict over sex.

The problem is that the male may just be wanting to be affectionate for affection's sake, and he is now being routinely shut down. He feels rejected, he feels hurt, and the more negative side of him comes out in their relationship. This makes him look like the bad guy. This compounds the problem tenfold, as she now feels even more pressure, so she continues to withdraw. You can imagine the damage this does to day-to-day connection. This sexual battleship dynamic is sadly all too common.

SEXUAL PROBLEMS AND FIXES

There are myriad problems that can happen in the bedroom.

Men may have **erectile dysfunction** – difficulties getting an erection and maintaining one – or experience **premature ejaculation**. These problems may have a medical basis, but commonly stem from pressure that men experience and can put on themselves. A man may feel that he has to perform, that he fears failure, that others are judging him. All this pressure causes problems with erection function. Of course, it is crucial to check out physical causes with your general practitioner. Women can have the female equivalent, called **vaginismus**. This is where, due to anxiety and pressure in their headspace, the vagina can be constricted and not release lubrication, both of which cause pain during penetration. The woman's vagina is saying, 'The world is a dangerous place, keep the barrier up' (their vagina struggles to have the capacity to relax and open with sexual intercourse).

Often men and women who are anxious due to historical trauma or just within themselves have these sexual difficulties. Sexual problems are sexual self-esteem problems. The answer is deliciously fun. Stop. Slow it down. Go back to your adolescent process of sexual discovery. We want to take away the pressure of intercourse and sex. We want to feel confident and in control. We want to reconnect with the tantalising sensations of simple touch and refine where our erogenous zones are and what we find most stimulating.

What to do? Here is the plan – it is a bit of a playful mystery hunt that could be explored in any relationship. The strategy involves banning sex during the start of this 're-connecting with your sensual self' process.

The first month, we return to first base. We return to just kissing and clothes-on touch. We stay here for a month. We are on an exploration journey, enjoying our lips, neck, throat, touching our fingertips, holding hands. We hug. We want more during this month, but we cannot go further. The goal is to feel a bit crazy here, building up to the desire for more, but not being able to go to second base. We also have no pressure. No pressure to have sex or get overtly sexual. This is tantric pleasure.

The second month, we can progress to touch with no clothing, but no orgasm-inducing touch. This is a sneaky second base. We can touch everywhere, but not with any active movement towards any climax behaviour.

No building up or orgasmic crescendo. No oral sex. This is just a touching and caressing stage. This is about touch for touch's sake. Not for orgasmic intention. We are exploring each other's bodies. Exploring the spots that drive us crazy just to be touched.

The third month is foreplay with no penetration. Touch, engage in oral play, explore. Remember, you are in control. This is about the two of you progressing only when the two of you are there together wanting this progression. Discover the pleasures without intercourse. Orgasm is perhaps the outcome, but not the goal. Enjoying the process, the wandering together.

The fourth month, again if you decide to advance, is the full smorgasbord. Hopefully by now you will have learnt to enjoy the entree, the sides, the ambience, the intimate embrace and personal conversation. This is about loosening up your headspace and savouring touch and exploration. Slow, slow, slow. Slow it down. Enjoy yourself and each other.

CHAPTER 12
PATIENCE AND TOLERANCE

Patience is a form of wisdom, and our people give us plenty of opportunity to practise this most valued virtue. Patience is the capacity to tolerate a challenging situation and challenging people. To keep your calm; to act, rather that react. Patience is often the best gift we can give our loved ones, our colleagues and our community.

On the flipside, intolerance of others usually comes from fear. Fear of difference, fear of being out of control, fear of someone getting in our way – which relates to fear of failure, or fear of loss of control again. We are often wound-up pressure cookers ready to go off, and people can get in our way or be an inconvenience. This can be our family, our children, our work colleagues, our community, or the checkout worker at our local store. Anyone.

Ironically, we only learn patience from first not having it, and then learning to extend it. Ideally, we learn this in childhood and teen years, but at any point in adulthood we can catch up on this learning curve. If you do not have a significant head injury causing impulsivity, you can tame your reactivity and your irritable response. As an adult you can learn to become patient. Through practice, like a muscle, our patience strengthens and extends; we can be patient for longer, and be patient despite outside pressures. The more we practise this skill, the more it grows. We need exposure and a clear desire to be patient. And we need practice. It is our loved ones and our outside world that give us this practice!

THE NEED TO FAKE PATIENCE

Then there is the art of faking. Sometimes we've just got nothing left. We are tired and we have pushed all day. We are now functioning on cortisol, our cranky stress hormone, and it is physiologically near impossible to feel patient. We are done. We may have a tight timeframe to work with and low energy, and yet we need to be patient with our people.

When we just have no patience left, this is where we fake being patient. We need to superimpose patient behaviour. We do this at work when we just have to be professional despite how we feel. Or we may do this when we are with strangers. We are capable of faking patience. It is just that we have to will ourselves to do it. Just *act* patient; it is close enough. Behave as if you are in good form. You will get through your tough situation, at minimum, without making the situation worse.

Even the process of faking requires us to force patience. We have to stop and breathe. This is good; this is more practice. Patience is a superpower that we need to really value and decide to identify with. We need to insist on this: the best version of ourselves. Your people will thank you for it. Part of patience is of course continuing to master being mindful of our minds and bodies in that moment. We are being mindful in order to be patient. Well done! Great effort!

CHAPTER 13
SINGLENESS

Of course, our single years have the potential to be a time of working out who we are, and how we want to approach our lives as an expression of ourselves. I see clients presenting with two types of problems related to singleness.

The first problem is the stigma that can surround being single. When asked what we are up to in life, why is there a dark cloud over replying, 'I'm single'? If we said, 'I'm recalibrating', or, 'I'm growing', or, 'I'm investing in myself', perhaps we would get a better response and we would not speak about our single status so timidly. It's wonderful being single; you can choose what you do next and with whom. You cannot launch into a healthy relationship until you are single. You are creating space and a foundation in your life from which to launch.

The second problem is that the single world is a secret society. Single people who want to meet someone don't automatically know who else is single, and so they have to work it out in their interactions. How exhausting and daunting. Perhaps this is one reason for our prolific use of internet dating, where we have a predefined group of (supposedly) single people. Half our work is done. I would not want to go around enquiring about people's relationship status; that's getting personal pretty quick.

Internet dating is great, by the way, for making first introductions. Dating is a numbers game; you have to keep going until you hit a bingo, and internet dating accelerates the process. But it is best to use it purely to set up a first meeting. As stated earlier, you don't actually date online; you need to be face to face to gauge your connection.

CHAPTER 14
LONELINESS

A brief word on loneliness. Clients often present with loneliness. Either they cannot tolerate being alone when their loved ones are elsewhere, or they feel loneliness as one of the driving forces to find their life partner.

Firstly, there is a skill in being able to sit with ourselves and enjoy our own company. Loneliness is a natural human state. It is perhaps a primary force in kicking us in the butt to find a loved one and to get amongst our friends and family. This is a healthy incentive. Loneliness has a healthy role to play in our motivation, and as social and interpersonal beings. But when we fret about loneliness, when we cannot make the most of the chapters in our life when we are alone with our own company, this can be a significant problem. The skill is to celebrate our time to ourselves; it is a resource to be used well. We need to make the most of the chapters in our life where we are having some 'island' time.

Many people feel a sense of emptiness when they are alone. They find this intolerable. Weekends are dreaded because they do not have the distraction and the structure of work. They look for tasks to fill their time and ease the loneliness. But when we cease to fear our solitude, we can start to realise that this is a time for creativity, for shaping our world on our terms, for having some time to work on our relationship with ourselves.

This is a time to come home to yourself. To literally sit with yourself and not be caught up in the influence or momentum of another. It is during these times of solitude and even silence that we can check ourselves out. It's like a personal retreat or boot-camp. This is challenging because keeping order in our mind is difficult. This is why we feel often more comfortable with external goals and stimulations to keep our attention elsewhere, to distract us from ourselves. When we are not distracted, we are more likely to worry, and our mind can become invaded by negative thoughts that control our consciousness. Worries about our job, our looks, our health, our relationships, our finances, our family, our long to-do list. When we are left with our thoughts – *boom!* – our mind scans for things to worry about. This is our challenge. Time for a spring clean; time to learn to rationalise and quieten our thoughts. Becoming skilled in this process is perhaps the main purpose of this whole book.

I'm not saying that you are not going to feel lonely and that you are not going to work towards bringing someone into your life. That is a great plan and focus. I'm saying in the meantime, when you are at this 'between' stage, *you are not just waiting*. You need to see it as a stage of *being*, of recalibrating. This is a life chapter for you. Use it, savour it, invest in it, celebrate it. Take your lonely state when and as it rises with a calm acceptance. Understand it is okay and a natural response, park it sideways, and get into your life.

CHAPTER 15
BREAKING UP HEALTHILY

One of the biggest heartaches in life is the break-up of a relationship. Society has such an obsession with romantic love that people can become distracted from learning to love themselves and therefore be very vulnerable in a break-up. This means that when we experience a break-up we can feel devastated and alone to such a degree that we can fall into a state of despair. We can even lose sight of why life is worth living, or we can be so scared of our pain that we can impulsively reach for another to distract us and soothe our loneliness. This of course means that we are not mindfully and reflectively choosing our next life partner; we are playing Russian roulette, and even more pain is likely to come our way.

Breaking up is a transition process. A time of ambiguity and disorientation. We can often feel like we are at a threshold and completely overwhelmed and confused. We can feel in between places, and insecure in ourselves. The real challenge and hurdle facing us is that we continue to pine for our former partner. Perhaps they have broken up with us and we are in this situation against our will. Or perhaps we know that the break-up is a wise decision (whether theirs or ours), but although our head is on board, the heart remains attached. We have some emotional healing to do.

As we cannot control our feelings of attachment, we really need to just look after ourselves while we let go over time. When former partners are no longer part of our world, with time and distance we recover and disconnect from them. But this is the problem. With social media, exes are staying in touch. Breaking up healthily is about deciding to *create the conditions* to let yourself heal. This means stopping putting gravel in your wound (through engagement with your ex). If you remain invested in what your ex is doing, you are keeping them present in your mind. This is a disaster as far as healing goes. It is non-healing. You will remain stuck in this no-man's-land while you allow yourself to indulge in thinking and researching them, even seeing them. If you have a break-up, it is essential to send your ex to a distant land in your mind. You need distance. Create distance. Decide to let yourself heal. Leave them alone, move on to new horizons, your new world, your next chapter in life. Grab it and create this chapter with a vengeance.

Sometimes you are obliged to see your ex. Perhaps you work together, co-parent together or have the same friendship group. This is a very, very big problem and a genuine hurdle to manage. The key is boundaries. Create boundaries around the way that you see them. Avoid intimate settings and think twice about whether you really need to be in the same room. If you are co-parenting, boundaries in your contact is good for your children as well, as you can show them a clear picture that you have separated and that there are now different arrangements. This gives clarity in their understanding of what has changed so that they can process and adjust. If you are ambiguous and without boundaries with your ex, you will confuse yourself and your children. You will all find it difficult to grieve and get your heads around the situation enough to move forward.

Have a good read of the below chapter on grief, because if you are struggling through a significant break-up, this is what you are experiencing: grief. If a loved one has died, the world understands that you are grieving, but they often don't comprehend the degree that you feel lost at sea after a break-up. Our society is not great at being tolerant or patient with people who are in transition and in a state of confusion and unsettled emotion. There needs to be understanding and normalising of this grief process. Our emotional pain is an alert that we need to do some inner work on ourselves, some healing, recovery and growth. While we want to blame our ex for our pain and our bruised situation, they are not part of the solution, and we are not working on them. We need to work on ourselves.

If you yourself have chosen the break-up then you have probably already disconnected from your ex. You are ready to move forward without a continued attachment. You might continue to care for them and wish them well, but you are not pining for them. You have actually done your grieving for the attachment during the relationship, as you went through the hard times and grieved for how you thought it would be, or for the good opinion that you once had of your partner. What you are probably needing to recover from is purely the hurt and the contempt that you might feel for your ex. Staying in contact is not only taking the sticking plaster off slowly and painfully, but it can refuel hope and attachment, only to place you back at the beginning of needing to mentally and emotionally separate again.

Can I stay friends with my ex? I think we have watched too many sitcoms where, due to the limited characters on the show, exes revert to being friends in a short time. Yes, you can be friends with your ex, but only when you have had years of moving on and establishing yourself in new chapters in your life. But really, why would you want to be friends? You have separated for a reason. You were not good for each other. Also, your new partners are likely to feel justifiably unsettled and question why you want your ex in your life. There is the exception, and that is with former partners who have done no or minimal harm to each other, whose attachment just fizzled out on both sides. It was genuinely a mutual, amicable and peaceful separation. This is incredibly rare. But the truth is that in this situation, they have reverted to being friends during the relationship, and then have just declared this 'friend zone' a reality with the break-up. Don't hold your breath for this break-up. Better odds to get a lotto ticket.

Whether you have initiated the break-up or not, the elephant in the room is your need to grieve – to recognise the hurt that you are likely to feel post break-up. You do not want your future consumed by the contempt you might feel for your ex. You do not want to become one of those bitter people defined by a previous break-up. There is profound power in forgiveness, as outlined below, but for many reasons it is absolutely essential that you work through your hurt. Get clear in your understanding of what happened to cause the relationship break down – your role and their role. Be real, be honest. Work not to rewrite history in order to overly blame them or yourself. Try, try, *try* to be as objective and accurate as you can. It is only then that you can heal in a healthy way and learn from your experience.

Journalling is profound. Try it and you will discover this. It is difficult to get issues out of your head by just thinking them in circles. We feel release and clarity by talking our issues out with someone or writing them down. This is the brilliance of journalling; it is right there when you need it, it is private so there are no limitations on what you share, and you can vent, vent, vent until it is released. Using journalling to get the situation clear is also great. Write down the story of what has happened. Get it out of your head. Be thorough and detailed. Take the time you need.

It is also absolutely a gift to talk it out with someone else; you physically feel so much lighter after a big heart-to-heart. It can be also refreshing to have the injection of someone else's more objective opinion and input. I'm talking about solid, releasing conversations with support people. Choose rational, old souls who you feel safe with to talk to. Avoid the drama-driven people who inflame the pain and the hurt.

When you feel that you have processed the break-up and released the hurt, and you think that you understand as much as you will be able to, then you need to *decide that your work is done*. You have passed the deadline for the past. You are now focused on the future. You are drawing a line.

Imagine yourself on an island. On this island is all of your healthy people; it is your safe place. It is where you are recuperating and rebuilding in preparation to launch into your next chapter. Then every time your ex comes to your mind and you lament how he or she hurt you ('I can't believe she did that', 'They have taken so much from me'), then you catch yourself and say to yourself, 'They are not welcome on my island.' You mentally swipe them to the side, away from your focus. You then distract yourself with something engaging so that your mind is not free to continue thinking about them. You are training your mind to say, 'I am not investing any more energy into my ex. I am not letting my ex hijack my mental health, my focus, my mood or my energy for the day.'

These are clear boundaries within yourself. This is a conscious decision to heal. This is intention and action.

It is extremely exciting and encouraging to then see the sheer number of thoughts about your ex drop away as you keep refusing to fuel these old neural pathways.

As time passes, yes, your ex will pop into your mind, of course. But you just reply, 'You are not welcome on my island', and then distract yourself with another activity or thought. Repeat and repeat and repeat. It is wonderful that you can liberate yourself from your ex.

But remember, this is only healthy if you have done your head and heart work first. Otherwise you would just be shutting down raw, unprocessed thought – a practice called **suppression**. This is like putting a lid on a volcano; it is going to build and cause harm to you in the future in a more pressured way. The hurt will also seep out in other ways, causing you harm. So ensure that you really do process the pain as honestly as you can before you expel your ex from your life.

This might sound strange, but it really is an investment in your future to have your first significant relationship break-up done, recovered, and behind you. Of course there are those who really get stuck in their grief here, which is extremely difficult for them. The vast majority, however, do heal, learn and eventually strengthen. This is because this experience teaches us that with time we can recover. Before our first break-up we have not experienced the grief process that comes with the end of a romantic relationship, which is a process of intensifying and then releasing. We climb up the mountain of grief (claw our way!), but then we *can* come down the other side and recover. Yes, we develop some emotional bruises, but all in all, in time and with a healthy approach, we can heal and move forward.

Our emotional bruises are really a sign of intelligence. We have been hurt and we want to prevent being hurt again. This makes sense. The problem is that we are often irrational in how we encode dangers into our life experience, and we also make drastic generalisations that are, again, not rational. One hurtful person can lead us to assume everyone could or would hurt us. This is an understandable knee-jerk reaction, but it's not rational and not helpful.

I expect that I will be sadly happy when our boys go through their first significant relationship break-up. Their pain will pain me, but I hope and believe that they will learn they can recover. With this life lesson, they can be less fearful of loss in their future, because they can learn that grief is a process, and that the second stage of the process is recovery and growth.

CHAPTER 16
MAKE FORGIVENESS YOUR SUPERPOWER

What happens to us in life is not as important as our response to it. What matters is our attitude in our response. Our negative experiences in life knock us around, bruise us, stop us in our tracks, but our responses decide whether we grow from them or decay.

Enter forgiveness. Forgiveness is not a religious concept. It is a skill essential to being an effective and adaptive human. This is ultimately something we do for our benefit, not others. This sounds horribly blunt and selfish, but it is true. Let me explain.

Holding on to anger is like drinking poison and expecting the other person to die.
Buddha

Forgiveness is releasing a grievance that we are actually entitled to have. Forgiveness is not forgetting. Forgiveness is not reconciliation. Forgiveness is the gift of true healing for ourselves. Forgiveness involves acknowledging that we have been harmed by another, and letting go our resentment or our wishes for retribution. This requires a high order of ethical and emotional maturity. We are liberating ourselves from oppressive bitterness and embracing our capacity for change; we begin to have choice over our attitude towards our present and our future. Our time, our future and our headspace are precious; it is essential that we do not overlay them with regrets, recriminations and bitterness. Forgiving can of course also vastly improve your relations with the forgiven person, and this can make your life easier.

Forgiveness involves an exercise of our consciousness. It requires determination. It is our superpower that combats and defeats the feelings of helplessness and anxiety that so routinely come during our times of conflict, loss and hurt. Our challenge is to remain hopeful while we are wrestling with life's inevitable losses. This is about the *meaning* that we assign to our experiences.

Why is it so common for people to hold on to – even passionately embrace – bitter thoughts about their past? There are some powerful reasons. First of all, forgiveness feels unjust; the person does not deserve our forgiveness. Forgiveness undermines our desire to punish the offender, and it takes away our sense of entitlement to righteous anger. Forgiveness blocks the revengeful feelings that we feel are natural and our right. Another problem is that we are naturally wired to feel resentment, so in order to forgive we need to take control of our thoughts rather than be on autopilot. The human brain has evolved so that we pay attention to negative thoughts and emotions that alert us to danger, rather than growing and building positive thoughts and emotions.

Our memories of emotional injuries or unfairness or rejection can sometimes become grievances that we hold onto with bitter determination. This can cause us to become preoccupied with the person or the group who has done us wrong. With a tight grasp, we hold them responsible for our unhappiness. The divorcee who fills his thoughts with his ex-partner's betrayal and lying, and the employee who ruminates about being unfairly moved from his job are showing bitterness. Intense and frequent negative thoughts about the past provide the raw material that blocks our ability to feel contentment and peace of mind.

Then there are the professional lamenters. You know when you talk with someone and they speak with such heat and explosive agitation, even hatred, and you think, *Wow, it's horrible that this is happening to you right now?* And then you find out that the hurt was inflicted ten years ago, not last month? A classic example is a person feeling bitterness towards an ex. They have shaped their world and their self-concept around this bitterness, and it has become part of their identity. The relationship can be like a painful movie they replay over and over again. They replay all the old stories, all the drama, all the misery.

They are stuck; they are defined by their past hurt. This is a very sad situation.

Our culture contributes to this. We live in a culture where everyone seems to have a sense of being wronged. If we blame every misfortune on others, we do not have to face the difficult task of examining how we have contributed to the situation or consider our capacity to respond in a healthy way. A difficult reality that we often push away is that life has always been and will always be full of adversity, difficult times and difficult people. What are we achieving here by not forgiving?

> An angry and hateful mind is a suffering mind.

As a motivation, perhaps notice how holding onto resentment affects your own mind, your mood and your body. Do you feel the tension in your body? Imagine the impact on your internal systems. Stress affects our immune system, our risk of cancer, our cardiovascular system, our blood pressure, our stress hormones and our nervous system. This is not to mention our capacity to engage in our relationships at home and work. We are limping along when we are disabled by a resentful outlook. Resentment has a venomous effect on your health and well-being. An angry and hateful mind is a suffering mind. We must *always* prioritise neutralising this resentment. What is the point of holding onto our hurt and our outrage? In doing so, we are hurting and burying *ourselves*, not the person who harmed us.

We have a choice here. The most crucial point is that when we keep placing responsibility onto others, we miss out on the ability to heal ourselves. It is profoundly empowering to learn and comprehend that *we* hold the key to determine whether we return from our struggles buoyant and afloat, or remain continually underwater, drowning in our hurt. The attitude that we adopt – our skill in forgiveness – is one of our superpowers.

> *Hatred never ceases by hatred;*
> *it only ceases by love.*
> *This is a timeless truth.*
> Ancient Buddhist Proverb

Forgiveness can feel impossible until you do it. Perhaps forgiveness is the most difficult of our human endeavours. Actually, I would argue that of all skills we can learn, this is the one that requires the most insight, but with this dedication comes the most extraordinary reward: freedom. Freedom from the pain of your past, and freedom to move forward and away from the hurt. Freedom to be yourself and not be shaped or shackled by the harm inflicted on you by others. This is profound reward for your insight and your efforts.

How do you forgive? Great question. The answer is by having understanding and compassion. Compassion is not only an intelligent and accurate response, but it is the opposite to bitterness. They are opposite sides of the same coin. When you think and feel with compassion, it is impossible to feel bitterness and hatred. They cancel each other out. Compassion creates forgiveness. Compassion towards the person who has harmed us is the antidote that stops them from continuing to harm us.

It is ironic; let's break it down. Compassion is looking at their situation and seeing the sadness in it; it is *feeling* for them. We turn our brain to contemplate their world. You can think of them as unskillful, lacking in insight and lost. Their actions are probably based on fear. You can start to understand the feelings and needs behind the words and actions of these difficult people.

Think about it: if a person goes around being harmful to others, they are not going to be able to build up healthy relationships. They are not going to experience the joy and connectedness of a healthy relationship. True, *true* joy comes from having a loving relationship with others – and they are missing out on this joy. This is where, instead of looking at them with angry eyes, we look at them with saddened eyes, for the reality that they are making for themselves.

Yes, we have been harmed by them. Yes, we may have emotional trauma. They may have led us into bankruptcy, we may have lost things and people very dear to us, but *they're* not sitting in a plum position either. Because what ultimately matters, more than what they have taken from us, is our peace of mind, our sense of purpose and our loving relationships. All of which they will not be able to achieve for themselves when they are going around with a corrupt moral compass, taking from the world and doing harm to others. Basically, they are left with their own company and the legacy they continue to create for themselves. This is very sad. When we see that they are left with themselves, we realise that the ultimate consequence is with them, not us. And with this understanding and compassion for them, our bitterness cannot exist.

> There is no greater healing than to have compassion for those who have harmed us.

When we direct compassion towards people who have hurt us, we are able to begin to neutralise the toxic effects of harbouring resentment. Furthermore, we even need to wish for our difficult people to be healthy and safe from harm and fear. It may seem challenging, even impossible, to think and feel with compassion towards these people, but you have to keep focused on the reality that resentment has a toxic effect on your own health and well-being.

We can begin to neutralise these resentments by understanding that the other party is acting in a way that has an ugly root cause. Unkind behaviour usually has its roots in fear and lack of awareness. They are coming from an unhealthy place and, without genuine insight and capacity to take responsibility, they are going to continue on a pathway to a another unhealthy place. You understand this and feel sadness for them. This is how we cultivate compassion for them. We then release the bitterness that we feel, we move forward, and the weight lifts. This is why we feel compassion for them: it helps us both.

Another important point is that you cannot go down the path of forgiveness grudgingly, as this will not set you free from your bitterness. Compassion is a shift in your perspective about the situation, a shift in your mindset. It is actually about letting go of this grudge that has you looking with a narrow focus on the specific harm caused to you.

Forgiveness is not about making excuses for the person's actions. We are not minimising or erasing the harm. Actually, forgiveness is the opposite. It is broadening our understanding and fully holding the person responsible for their actions and being upfront and clear about the situation and the harm caused to you. It is understanding what was happening for the person when they made their choices to hurt you. It is then having understanding and compassion that this is messy and harmful to the other person's own well-being, and is likely to continue to be harmful to them. This is a sad situation for them, and you can connect with their sadness; you think and feel empathetically. Your eyes are open to a 360-degree view of their situation.

Just remember that forgiving does not involve suppressing bad memories. If you make explicit attempts to suppress your thoughts it will backfire and actually increase the likelihood of imagining the forbidden topic. Remember the pink rabbit that was mentioned earlier (Chapter 8 of this book, and Book 1, Chapters 24 and 31)? If you put energy into not having a thought, your brain gives attention to that thought and it keeps returning. (Try it! For the next five minutes, try not to think of a pink rabbit.) In contrast, forgiveness leaves the memory intact but removes and works to transform the sting. It is a rewriting strategy that broadens the information to include the offender's background and future.

Forgiveness doesn't mean that you should or need to reconcile or bring down your boundaries or have this person in your world. It is purely about your mindset towards them. They do not need to know your mindset. This is not about telling them of your forgiveness or compassion. It is not a case of forgiving others for their sake. This is purely a personal process for your own benefit. This is not about being selfish; this is about self-care. Out of duty of care to ourselves it is of paramount importance to have very firm boundaries with people who have harmed you. Fortified boundaries and compassion and forgiveness can all coexist. They are separate issues and processes.

CHAPTER 17
WOMEN RISE BY VALUING OTHER WOMEN

Women can be strange creatures; in truth we are all strange creatures. But the cliché of women being complicated is very true, I think.

When men look to other men and see something they admire, they make a note of it, almost as if they are window shopping for ideas, while women can tend to attack other women. *Not always, of course,* but much too often.

When women see strengths in other women, they sometimes feel hostility. They can take it personally and compare themselves. They can feel inferior in that moment. So what do they do? They can be bitchy towards each other. I'm talking very broadly here; there is a percentage of women who do not do this, and a percentage of men who do.

Why do we do this? Perhaps it is the threads of our history that still hold us. We only need to go back in history, when in many cultures women were treated as possessions. The main resource available to them for survival was how they compared to other women on the marriage market. So sad. So true. So were women therefore going to celebrate other women? No, they were in competition for survival. If the women did not marry well, their future was not secure.

At social gatherings sometimes you might observe a sharp division and grouping of women into the 'stay-at-home mums' and the 'working mums', with women in each group casting disapproving glances at the other. They feel threatened and jealous of each other. In truth, they are probably having feelings of guilt triggered within themselves. The stay-at-home mums fear they should be working, and the working mums fear they should be staying at home. They are judging themselves and assuming that they are being judged at the same time. What a mess. What a circus. Aren't we all ridiculous? Let's all just take a breath!

Women attack women.

Well it's time to wake up, move on, spring clean these cobwebs. *Women need to learn to celebrate and get inspiration from each other, and not compete with each other.* It is extraordinary how much harm women do to each other. The schoolyard bullying against girls from elementary to high school, I would argue, is mostly from other girls. This is where the bitching culture starts. Not everyone is involved, but the emphasis on image and social status and inclusion can be paralysing for our poor teen girls.

I have observed in session that women in their mid-thirties finally start to figure it out; they begin to cut the crap and become strengths to each other. Sadly, it is during the earlier formative years that we throw barbs and spears at each other, and these are the crucial years when we need to learn our positive self-talk, our self-worth and our unique personal expression. We could call the time before our mid-thirties the 'female civil war period', our inter-female bitchy culture. It is nothing but cruel.

A strong sense of female camaraderie would change our world. Literally. We would stop fighting amongst ourselves and start to look outward. We could build and celebrate each other's strengths and celebrate, focusing on what actually matters: big life and big world issues. Perhaps save the planet – again, *literally*.

> A strong sense of female camaraderie
> would change our world.

Another related issue is that women often communicate in a different way from men, and they don't have a clue they are doing it. I used to work in academic circles, and when I marked student papers, I saw first-hand how gender often affected writing styles. Broadly speaking, the males would write on point about the topic, and were direct and clear. The females tended to cushion the language, almost apologising for the statements they put forward. Women also struggle to talk confidently about themselves; they can minimise and put themselves down, they can be deferring in their manner, as if they have travelled in time back to the Victorian era. Women are getting better at advocating for their pay levels, but there are mountains yet to be climbed here. When will women be on par with men in terms of their ability to state their fair claim to pay negotiations? We have a way to go.

CHAPTER 18
SEXISM CONFUSES ME

I grew up in a strange, experimental environment, it seems. It was just my sister and I growing up with our beautiful mother in our primary home. I would visit my father's house, but it was not my home; I do not recall having any personal belongings there. In my personal home, gender was not a factor; it was not brought to my attention. Our family (and friends) never let gender play a role in chores, future options, aspirations or ways of relating. So I was blessed and grew up unaware of sexism, or of restrictions placed on men or women based on their gender.

It was therefore a shock and piercingly obvious when I went on to have snippets of exposure over time. For example, I used to visit the house of a friend whose parents seemed to be lost in time, saturated in 1950s gender stereotypes. I felt like an alien looking in on these strange creatures and their absurd, ignorant, limiting and oppressive behaviours towards females *and* males. This strange and scripted behaviour made no sense to me, and I recall it was jarring to witness. This was one of my first studies of human behaviour.

I have immense respect for the women's movement, as well as the awakening of men to emotional intelligence and expressiveness. I don't recall being on the receiving end of gender bias; however, I have not had any early conditioning to be submissive to men. As a result, when as an adult I have had moments of exposure to attempted gender oppression, I have found it peculiar, even comical, and I have flicked it sideways and bulldozed forward as if it didn't exist, thereby giving it no power. I think confidence in this way is contagious, and sexist behaviours are actually quite feeble. They can crumble when you eyeball them with a sensible, grounded approach.

This of course could be extremely difficult for someone who has grown up with gender bias and oppression. For them, they would need to learn to separate themselves away from the gender messages that they perhaps grew up with. They would need to re-invent the wheel and decide for themselves that they are not going to be defined or restricted by gender. They may even need to learn to celebrate their gender. I truly admire those who have had to move out of the shadow of sexist views. Having this background would indeed be a challenge in learning to redefine yourself and your own independent life views.

Let's be clear however, the solution does not lie in the woman's attitude to sexism. Globally, women can brush rude, ignorant comments aside, but it won't alter the fact that women continue to get paid less than their male colleagues, or that in some countries their freedoms are severely restricted, their rights suppressed. Sexism continues to cause serious harm in our world. The solution involves addressing the root value system that continues to grow this gender bias.

When someone tries to dominate another, it says that they are not confident. An internally confident person has no reason to dominate another. I celebrate the genders; we need to understand them and embrace all of the gender strengths. Women may be strong because they are strong as women; they do not need to become more male to have strength. We celebrate and embrace our own necessary mix of masculinity and femininity, no matter our gender. We do not paint the rainbow with one colour; we celebrate the variety of colours and the way they complement each other – how they need each other to really shine.

CHAPTER 19
FAMILY

Some of the most meaningful and intense experiences in our lives are the result of family relationships. Adult life successes usually pale in comparison to family connectedness.

What is a family? When we are younger, we usually think of our literal family unit in which we were raised. As we get older, we realise that our family are people who we bring into our lives in addition to our biological family. We adopt people throughout our lives; we come upon gems and bring them into the centre of our world, or we outsource when a role needs to be filled.

As a child, I adopted our neighbour Steve as my father figure. From the age of six through to twelve (we moved house when I was twelve), I would scale our six-foot fence and hang out with Steve. Steve is a beautiful soul; he and his wife could not have children and he adopted me right back. He would stop whatever he was doing, and we would just talk and potter together. We still talk today with such ease, love and connection. Children are extraordinary. They can read people, and know when they have hit gold. They know when they have needs that are not being met and they outsource. It could be a teacher, an aunty, a neighbour. A resilient child outsources.

Our family is perhaps our most important social environment, and our ability for our family interaction to be meaningful and rich is therefore of profound importance. It is no secret that there is a huge range in types of family relationships. Some family relationships are playful and joyful, some warm and supportive, some mundane and boring, some very demanding and challenging, and some dangerous to our emotional safety. It is within families that the rate of murder and child abuse is highest. These are scary facts. Some family relationships can make us profoundly rich with love, joy and connectedness, while some family relationships can be burdensome and even traumatic. The quality of family relationships really comes down to the family members' mental health, moral values and altruistic intent towards one another.

But let's just turn to the typical family situation, where there is love and there are no extreme violations or harm to one another. The danger with the average family is complacency. As stated earlier, allowing complacency is like not watering the plant that is the family, and not noticing as it withers to a shadow of its potential. This is the family in which there is not abuse, but there is neglect.

Those have most power to hurt us, that we love.
– from *The maid's tragedy* by Francis Beaumont and John Fletcher, playwrights

If you want a thriving home life, if you want your family to respect you – to actually *want* your company – you need to nurture your family relationships. When it comes to family relationships, you get out what you put in. You cannot 'set and forget' with family; you cannot park them while you get on with martyring yourself with your work role, workload, or personal interests. Because one day you will come home and the family will not be there. They may be there in body, but not in connection, and you will be strangers or even foes.

All of the chapters in this book can be applied to our family, our children, partners, siblings, parents, grandparents, nephews and nieces. What is the goal for your family? What kind of family relations do you want? What family rituals do you want? What family culture do you want? How do you spend quality time doing quality things with your family members? Are you an expert in knowing your family members – their lives now, their history, their personalities, their challenges and aspirations? Step back and ask these questions. We cannot move forward if we do not know where we are going. We cannot expect to get there until we grab our oars and start paddling. We need to prioritise and put in effort.

So wake up, step up, and *grow your family*. Don't be asleep to your family slipping into the silent creep of disintegration.

CHAPTER 20
LGBTQIA, CELEBRATING OUR INDIVIDUALITY

We can never hide a part of ourselves, not if we want to be healthy, grounded and have a lightness in our being. Our sexual orientation and our gender identity are core to who we are. These are what make us. We are all different, and we are all supposed to be different. We need to appreciate and celebrate our individuality. When people fear difference, this is due to their personal insecurity and ignorance.

Whenever we hide anything from anybody, it means we are scared, and we are worried about what someone else is going to think of us. We need to be proud of who we are and live our truth. Our challenge is living true to ourselves and learning not to worry about what other people think. In truth, this is about developing the personal strength to not be as affected by others' ignorance and persecution. This is a life's work; we never truly arrive. After all, we are human and vulnerable, and we just want to be loved and accepted.

When we have a child who is LGBTQIA, we need to embrace who our child is, celebrate them and not want to change them for a second. Then, as their family, it is our responsibility to be their grounding force and to support them, when the world might not be as awake and evolved. The hardest periods in our life often end up being the most defining, the best parts, the times when we made ourselves who we are through our honest expression of our gender and our sexuality. We can realise our strength. We can realise our kindness and compassion towards ourselves and our people. It is during these times that we grow.

So to grow we have to face our fears. We do not grow when we avoid and run away; we only prolong the fight. It is through these tough times that we become proud of who we are. The process of embracing our sexuality and our gender and the sexuality and gender of our children is one of these growth times, whether we like it or not. It is a time of finding our feet, finding our voice. This is also the time for us families to embrace and hear and understand our loved ones. We all need to be recognised for who we are.

CHAPTER 21
TRICKY TRAUMATIC PEOPLE IN OUR WORLD: PROFILING

Some people are just difficult; they are hard work. They can be insensitive, irresponsible, pushy, demanding, threatening and unco-operative. Some problem people are driven by their ego and power; they are threatened by other people's strengths and they work to cut them down. They are not **affiliation orientated** – in other words, they don't draw upon and celebrate other people's strengths as they work collaboratively. They are instead **power orientated**. They will climb on top of you and exploit you to get where they want to go (up the food chain, for sure).

Sometimes people who are closest to us are actually those who are causing us the most stress and harm. We have no choice but to learn a lot about ourselves when faced with these tricky people. We learn about our unmet needs, our easily-pressed buttons, our coping mechanisms – good or bad – and how good our skills of emotional regulation are. Tricky people force us to develop our interpersonal mindfulness and eventually our assertiveness skills.

While you may be able to see that the tricky person is acting out of insecurity and limited skill, it is important to have good boundaries to protect yourself from harm. The need for and the skill of having boundaries is covered below, while the focus here is the skill of **profiling**.

If someone has a history of behaving poorly in a certain way, wouldn't it make sense to protect yourself from future repeats of the same hurtful behaviour? This is what profiling is. It is using previous behaviour to anticipate possible future behaviour from tricky people. It is about acknowledging patterns of previous behaviour that are likely to repeat. It is *not* condoning this behaviour in any way. When we can easily anticipate a repeat of poor behaviour, we prove to ourselves that the issue is not us, and we can distance ourselves from their reactivity because it is just so predictable. Actually, if we feel disappointed by a hurtful behaviour it is evidence that we have not done the head work of preparing our expectations, of profiling. We need to acknowledge patterns before they repeat.

A fun random thing that you can do to keep lightness in you throughout this process and to prevent you from getting too caught up in others' tricky behaviour is to actually put in a bet of how many times during a coming interaction the tricky person is going to behave badly. For example, if the person likes to take your disclosure and flip it to make it about them, you could count how many times she does this. You are so busy watching and counting that you, on the one hand, can see how absurd their behaviour is and, on the other hand, can keep yourself distracted. You're focusing on your task of counting rather than on the hurtful content of their conversation. Brilliant! Go and practise with your tricky person. Become an expert profiler with tricky people in your life.

When we have a tricky person in our life, one of our challenges is to grieve for the healthy relationship that we wish we could have had with them if they were healthy. This is a type of grief, don't mistake it. We often have an ideal family image in our minds, but then in contrast we have our actual family with the tricky members who seem incapable of having a healthy, safe relationship. We need to grieve for our ideals as we accept our reality. This allows us to scavenge through and find and engage with their positive aspects, while maintaining boundaries for the unhealthy, negative parts of their behaviour.

CHAPTER 22
NARCISSISTIC PERSONALITY DISORDER

Do you know what **narcissistic personality disorder** is? If you don't know, or your knowledge is limited, best to skill up. Knowing how to recognise someone with narcissistic personality disorder could save you a lot of trauma and heartbreak.

Once you see the pattern of narcissistic personality disorder, you can't unsee it. You have joined the portion of the population who are initiated in this skill. Narcissistic personality disorder (NPD) is a diagnosis; it is a personality disorder categorised in the DSM5, the diagnostic manual used by psychologists, psychiatrists and other doctors. There is a similar diagnosis in the European diagnostic manual, the ICD10.

NPD is different to just **narcissism**, which involves being self-centred and egotistical. Narcissism is actually part of a healthy developmental stage in early childhood during which we feel omnipotent in our world. It is normal for infants to feel and perceive that they are the centre of the universe and their adults' world. One could humorously argue that narcissistic personality disorder is when we get stuck at this early childhood stage of self-centredness and tantrums, but it is much more complicated than that.

Explains but does not excuse.

While narcissistic personality disorder is not that common (up to 1% of the population, more in males than females), people with this presentation cast a long shadow over the rest of the population. Let's refer to it as NPD from here on. It is wise to understand what NPD is. It is as if most of us are sheep, but when you experience someone with NPD in your personal life it is like coming across a wolf in sheep's clothing. The population seems to be divided into three groups: 1) those who have experienced someone in their life with NPD but have got through it and are now in an emotionally safe place; 2) those who are currently in the commotion of trying to manage someone with NPD in their life; and 3) those who are lucky enough not to have had life experience of someone with NPD. This third group is the majority of the population. They are the Little Red Riding Hoods of the world, wandering along naïve and therefore vulnerable. In my psychology clinic I have a disproportionately large percentage of the number 2 group who are currently traumatised by the NPD person in their life, in their family, their workforce or, to a lesser degree, in their friendship circle.

Narcissistic personality disorder is the epitome and the extreme of 'trickiness' a person can have. It involves a significant impairment in personality functioning. People with NPD are very insecure, and compensate by viewing themselves as exceptional, and being extremely self-focused. They cannot tolerate any criticism, routinely responding with rage if held accountable and made to face reality. They have very poor emotional regulation skills, and use frequent anger outbursts to control others. They are grandiose, have an inflated sense of themselves and are very image orientated. They present with superficial charm to impress others and draw them in. Once this façade drops, however, the behaviour is often manipulative, lacking in empathy and concern for others.

It is this manipulation that causes the damage to people in their world. Instead of learning to collaborate and communicate with mindfulness of others, they have become masters of what is now called 'gaslighting', as they twist the conversation and situation to punish the other party and take away their voice. NPD people often monopolise conversations and belittle others, believing they are inferior and treating them accordingly.

They are not astute at reciprocal loving relationships. Once the superficial charm has dropped, they are very 'taking', not giving. They take advantage of others. Of key importance is that people with NPD have very limited to no insight. They do not genuinely take responsibility for their actions, partly because their focus on themselves makes their insight limited, and partly because their impaired empathy reduces their motivation to take responsibility. The person with NPD works to undermine the other person's self-worth. Their relationships routinely meet the definition of a **domestic violence relationship**. If the partner ever manages to leave, they often end up with their self-esteem in a puddle on the floor.

> *The malignant narcissist, they are wired to win.*
> *Why are they the centre of the universe?*
> *You do not exist; you just exist for their needs to be met.*
> Carla, client

One rather creative analogy that I have used to help comprehend the nature of NPD is that of an egg. Stay with me.

With healthy personality development, you could think of us as being an egg that is boiled carefully and slowly over time. We are the egg, and our shell is our defences. Your personality (your boiled egg) becomes more solid with time; your goal is to learn about yourself and to learn to relate to others in a constructive way. Your shell (your defence mechanism) is therefore not actually needed to keep you functionally intact. You are able to open your shell and make and receive insightful comments. You are aware of what is going on, on a deeply personal level.

A person with NPD has *not* been cooking and developing from the inside out; they have instead been growing their shell. They have been learning how to manipulate others and often have a high level of verbal intelligence. Rather than learning to work alongside others, they have learnt how to confuse, deflect and blame others. Their shell is thick and seems impenetrable. Inside they are goo; they are very insecure and they are not solid within themselves. The thing is that their awareness of themselves is only on this outer shell level. They do not have self-awareness of their inner goo – no insight, no willingness or capacity to take responsibility for themselves – and if you breach their defences and peel back their shell with insightful comments, they respond with rage, a fearsome response designed to ward you off. They are not able to look inside their shell to their inner self, and you are forcefully stopped from getting this close. They never have insight that they actually have narcissistic personality disorder. An important trait of people with NPD is their superficial charm. This is their engineered social-image shell. At home, behind closed doors, this charm is eventually parked to the side, and it is only those in the immediate circle who then see the true nature of their personality and the behaviour.

When you have someone in your world with NPD, the boundaries discussed earlier need to be PROFOUND. You need to have very clear boundaries and accept that this is a *managed* relationship, not a relaxed, safe relationship. You will always need to be on duty, proactively profiling and expecting, so that you minimise the risk of being hurt.

Alternatively, you may decide that it is healthier not to have this person in your world at all. You might need to completely divorce them (sibling, cousin, uncle, friend), because they are so unhealthy and dangerous to your mental health. You are literally not emotionally safe with someone who wants to do you harm. If you're in a situation where a person means you harm – perhaps by oppressing you or manipulating you psychologically – then their behaviour would meet the criteria for domestic violence. If you do remove yourself from them, again your boundaries in implementing this withdrawal will need to be impenetrable. Once you have worked out your healthy balance for the future, you will have some work to do to recover from this traumatic relationship. This is a grief and acceptance process, which will be discussed in more depth in Book 6, Chapter 5.

CHAPTER 23
ABUSE

People who experience sexual and physical abuse spend much of their time talking with me in session about the psychological abuse component. I wouldn't say that psychological abuse is worse – that would be simplifying a very complex picture of trauma – but I would say that psychological abuse perhaps leaves the strongest imprint, the deepest damage. It is the undermining comments, the dismissive comments that say you are not important, and that you have no voice. It is the way that the situation and the blame is manipulated and twisted so that the victim is made to feel guilty.

This type of behaviour is now becoming more widely understood, and the phrase **'gaslighting'** is helping people to find words for their vague, very confusing experience. The gaslighter is supposedly our support person, but they do not actually support us. Rather, they abandon us and we learn the devastating lesson that we cannot trust them during our vulnerable times. We feel alone. We start to think of ourselves through the derogatory words used by the oppressor who has worked methodically to shred our self-worth and our sense of our own voice. This psychological abuse damages our learnt version of love, our ability to know secure attachment, and the foundation of our self-talk. We can easily become the wounded dog that either whimpers in the corner or growls at and bites anyone who tries to get close.

So what is domestic violence? Domestic violence is a situation in which a person inflicts psychological, verbal, physical, sexual or financial abuse on another, with an agenda to reduce the victim's sense of self and make their confidence dwindle and erode. The perpetrator methodically takes away the victim's voice and personal power, and it becomes the norm for them to inflict harm.

There is an interesting and sad pattern to abuse. When it is predictable it is less scary and we can strangely feel some level of control, because we can anticipate it and try to work around it – to minimise it, to dodge it, to protect ourselves. When it is unpredictable, however, it's much harder. We live on eggshells; we don't know when and what will happen. This is the most terrifying situation.

There is another pattern that leaves many trapped in the domestic violence cycle, and this is the perpetrator coming back and saying they are 'sorry', and that they will 'make it up to you'. We are so bruised in ourselves and so desperately wanting it to be okay, that we take this as a glimmer of hope and we think, *Maybe they will change and be different now*. But inevitably the merry-go-round continues, and once they are secure in the belief that you are not leaving, they drop their guard; any good behaviour is short-lived and the abuse repeats. The domestic violence cycle, however, has us so eroded and worn down that we feel too feeble and lost to leave.

With emotional support, financial options and enough personal hope and strength, many can leave an abusive relationship. This process involves feeling torn, as the primitive self may remain attached and the head has to work against the heart. The community needs to understand the complexity of the situation and the profound courage and strength that is needed to leave an abusive relationship. Please do not be quick to judge and simplify. The comment just leave' shows no awareness. We are a fly leaving a strong cobweb, and it is profoundly difficult, terrifying and exhausting. I warmly celebrate all who charge forward and recreate their lives with only healthy new-found family and friends. You are in the hero category to me.

CHAPTER 24
BOUNDARIES ...
ASSERTIVENESS

Do you want people to routinely treat you well? Do you want to experience the *best* of others? Do you want to create good habits in your relationships? A resounding 'yes', I am sure. Then **boundaries** are your best friend.

Setting boundaries is not a natural talent. This is a skill; it is like riding a bike: you learn it, you practise it, and then you are set for life. By the way, we are talking about being assertive with friends, co-workers, strangers, partners, family, children, clients, acquaintances – all human sentient beings!

There are three types of power relations: being **passive**, **assertive** or **dominant**.

Assertiveness is part of the eloquent art of self-care. It is drawing the line and communicating to others your expectations of how they need to treat you. When you have mastered assertiveness, you are being proactive and preventative in your life. Life gets pretty smooth from here because people routinely treat you well, as they are picking up on your gentle tone that this is what you expect of them.

People will give you what you expect of them.

Dominant people impose themselves and their needs on others. This is obviously not being mindful of others. It is shortsighted, as people will not tolerate this over time.

It's like stretching out a rubber band of entitlement and demanding more and more. It will in time fling right back at you. Dominant behaviour is not ultimately sustainable, as there is no balance. Something eventually gives and is lost.

Passive people tend to sit back and see how others treat them. They do not have the tendency to dominate others, so they expect others not to dominate them. They use their reference point to naïvely assume how others will be. It's strange, but those of us with a passive outlook really expect others to be clones of us. We are then taken aback and hurt when others are dominant towards us. We *receive* their behaviour.

But this is the thing: *we* are responsible for holding our assertive line; *we* are responsible for insisting that we only receive *assertive* behaviour from others, not dominant behaviour. We have to hold the line. Why? Because we set the bar for what we will tolerate from others, and usually the other party learns *from us* the 'norms' of how to treat us. Our assertiveness can keep dominant people in check, whether they are intentionally or habitually dominant.

More commonly dominant behaviour comes from absent-minded people who are not intent on dominating us; they have just slid into bad habits. Let's explain. Humans are complacent creatures. When we are given a level of generosity from others, over time we tend to habituate. We start to take what we are given for granted and, sadly, we come to expect it and then want even more. It is our job, therefore, to hold the line and not be taken for granted by others, even our loved ones.

I have a friend who I would regularly catch up with. I offered on the first few times to pick her up as I drove by. What do you think happened? Yep, she came to expect that I was the designated transport and if I couldn't or didn't pick her up, she would become put out and annoyed. So I consciously decided to shake it up, and I only offered to pick her up every second or third time we caught up. She learnt the new fairer breakdown and stopped presuming that I would be the transport. A simple but common example.

How do we be assertive? First of all, we have to work out if a line is being crossed. Where is our line? One way to work this out is to imagine that your positions were swapped with the other person. Would you ask of them what they are asking of you? If the answer is no, then it is probably not okay for them to behave that way towards you. You need to draw the line and diplomatically but assertively let them know that is not okay.

The second way to work out if their behaviour has crossed the line is to consider, 'Do I want this to become the norm between us?' If our other person behaves in a problem way several times, it is likely to become a habit. The behaviour locks into a norm between you. If you are not happy with this behaviour over the long term, then don't accept it in the short term, because habits form quickly.

We become complacent, and these habits are hard to change as we like to keep the status quo when it works for us. Remember, this is usually with no bad intent from them, just complacency.

An absolute classic example is house chores. If we start the habit of doing more than our partner or doing chores that our teenagers are capable of doing, then we are saying, 'Let's do this for the long term.' We then complain about how unfair the housework breakdown is when we have actually created the norm. So look around; what bad habits are you forming, or have you formed over the years? These are areas to become assertive with and to draw the line in.

Let's now talk about your language and manner in being assertive. Assertiveness is not about being dominant and it is not about being aggressive; you are not going to impose yourself on others. You are just not letting them impose themselves on you. Assertiveness is a gentle approach. It is a diplomatic tone; you are communicating with your actions or words with calmness, but quiet firmness. With your actions, you pull back from overcompensating for their inaction. You take your own plates from the table to the sink, not theirs. Or, to refer to my transport example, you politely make yourself less available, so that you are not responsible for all of the driving.

You can address the issue directly, or you can just be less available in what you give. When talking about the issue with your other person, make sure that you have kindness in your voice. It is essential that they do not see you as being conflictual. If we are at all aggressive in our tone, the other person puts their defensive walls up, and it becomes combative. Their ears close and they move to self-protection mode. Make it short and sweet and make a very balanced, non-emotional statement. For example, 'We both work full time, so I don't think it's fair that I cook and clean up the dishes. We can do one or the other; which would you like to do?' The key then is to stand by your assertion. Until you become practised, this will be uncomfortable for you. What is important to focus on through this is the longer-term habits you are creating. So don't cave, don't wash up if you have cooked. If you do cave, your behaviour is just saying that you will tolerate the imposing behaviour. You cannot say one thing and do another. You cannot rescue others from learning their own accountability for their actions. If your teenager needs to learn to wash her work clothes and you have addressed this, let her fall on her sword and not have her clothes washed on time. This is a cause-and-effect situation that she can learn from. Many mums in particular spend their time rescuing their family members from their own responsibilities. This just creates dependants, not capable young men and women.

We are, of course, also human. It's important to realise that *we* can become complacent too, and to catch ourselves. We need to remain mindfully grateful and not become spoilt. Otherwise we ourselves step over the line and start to presume too much of others. My beautiful Jon (yes, this is what I routinely call him) each workday morning gets up and makes me a coffee. I don't really know how this tradition started but I am not complaining. I love it. But what do I do? I have started to expect it; I look for it. I have become spoilt. So I consciously work to think, *He does not need to bring it each morning*, and to continue to see it as a bonus, a treat. I keep my 'thank yous' fresh and genuinely appreciative. This is a simple but good example.

A final point is that with assertiveness, our goal is not for our kids or our work colleagues (for example) to *like* us by seeking to please them. That's not assertiveness, it's permissiveness. Our goal is for them to *respect* us, and it means we are acting with self-respect – with assertiveness. Respect means having good boundaries and standards and being true to yourself. If they don't respect you then they can't really be valuing you. From respect comes the admiration and the liking that you seek.

CHAPTER 25
FRIENDSHIP

Make friends. Protect and nurture your friendships. Why? Because you are creating a protective circle around you to help you feel safe and valued. You can inspire each other, share stories and help each other through tough and healing times. Friendship is a source of intimacy; it is a connective thread that links us with our loved ones throughout our lives.

Many people believe that friendships, like families, just evolve – that they happen naturally. They also believe that if a friendship fails, it is out of their hands. The opposite is true, however; friendship is about prioritising and giving of yourself. Friendship is a skill in being awake and mindful of our close people. During childhood and adolescence, we are routinely surrounded by friends, spending hours together at school or at gatherings, often for many continual years, and with a lot of leisure and fun involved. This means that during our youth, making friends can seem like a spontaneous process. In adult life, however, friendships are cultivated; they are intentionally created as we have to make time for them and make them our priority.

Real friendship is an act of recognition. You know each other for who you are, and you cherish each other. The connection of friendship is not manufactured; it grows. We deepen and preserve our connections. They take creation and maintenance and energy. When we do not prioritise our friendships, we do not fuel them and we can become complacent and lazy with our loved ones. Then comes a day when we look up from our lives and exclaim, 'I have no friends!'

The worst solitude is to be destitute of sincere friendship.
Sir Francis Bacon, English philosopher

I think of making new friends as a hobby, an art form. You constantly have an eye out for people you are drawn to, who you feel safe with, who inspire you. Then you step out of your comfort zone and put in some effort. When you have become a little bit familiar with each other, you ask them if they would like to meet for a coffee. You let them know that you enjoy their company. They love this recognition of their value. Then you meet up, make sure the conversation is real and not light and superficial. Then through getting to know each other, and prioritising making time to meet up and enjoy each other's company, a friendship is formed. Keep fuelling it as a priority in your life, keep being real in your interactions, and a profound bridge will be built between you.

Many people worry when they catch up with friends that if they talk about their stuff, they will over-burden their special person. A few things to consider here. It's not great to be an overly negative person who routinely creates and loves drama; this is destructive and not good for anyone. So if this is your manner, many quality people won't stick around for the next episode of your soapie. But if you are sharing a validly distressing time with your friend and you have some relative balance to your approach, then you are pretty much going to be okay.

What is consuming in your world is not necessarily consuming to the other person. A 100% level of distress to you will only be perhaps 5% distress to them, because your friend is not living it. They are coming from an outsider's standpoint. So you do not really need to worry about over-burdening them. This is especially if you get a nice third/third/third ratio going. I would propose (very roughly and with a lot of flexibility) that you keep a third of your catch-up time light and fun, talk for a third of the time about *their* world, and the remaining third about *your* stuff. This keeps the serious chat balanced with the playful, fuelling chat, and it makes sure that the friendship keeps some form of balance. It makes it about the two of you, not one of you overshadowing the other, and keeps the heavy themes from bogging it down too much. Fun time is the balancer. Of course, during times of acute crisis and distress, the friendship is a safety net to catch us when we are falling, and the conversation is going to be about the person in the crisis state.

We truly are sloths when it comes to catching up with friends. We love them, we enjoy them, we say with absolute conviction and sincerity that we want to catch up with them, but we do nothing. We get caught up in our daily lives and the comfort of our own routine and our immediate family and work colleagues, and we often do not actually make time to catch up with our friends. Or if we do, it is rare. The exceptions tend to be the raging extroverts who need to be with people to refuel their energy reserves, or people who are in life transition and feel at a loose end. If we do not feel connected with our own lives and routine, we often become more proactive in looking to our people for companionship and to soothe us.

Once we realise that we are friendship sloths, we can consciously make sure that we don't take it personally when our friends don't follow up an invitation and they are slack. Look around; so are we. They're in all probability like that with everyone, not just you. The trick is to make their slackness work for you. I think it's great. Their inertia means that *I* get to organise my friends, decide who I would like to invite and make it happen. My friends actually say, 'So glad you have organised this; can you organise it next time – because you will, and I am pathetic at getting around to it.' I'm good with this. I know it's everyone's nature to get lost in their daily life. Myself included if I let it.

What sort of friend are you? There is no doubt that with our loved ones, we get out what we put in. The type of energy that you give out is the energy that you will receive from others because you tap into that same quality in them. If you are playful and positive, they are more likely to meet you with the same. If you are negative and critical, then you will cast a negative cloud and they will either readily join you (if they also are feeling negative) or look for opportunities to shut the conversation down early.

Friendship is about creating and living in our tribe. While it is crucial to be able to be yourself and enjoy your own company, friendship is also about taking care of each other. Real joy, humour and relief comes from tackling life together. We lift each other up and ground each other; we all gain. When we feel isolated, we naturally feel lonely. When we are not truly connected to others we can feel lonely even in a crowd of people.

You may notice that compared to family, friendships can be much easier to enjoy. This makes sense as we actually choose our friends because we are drawn to them, we enjoy them, find them inspiring and share their interests. Friendships can involve mysterious novelty, excitement, discovery and adventure. In a healthy version we are celebrated by our friends for who we are; we don't need to change ourselves, for our sense of our self is seen and valued.

There are of course destructive 'friendships'. This is when the term 'friendship' is used, but it is not really a true state. Sit back and see what is going on; if your 'friend' is validating your own insecure sense of yourself, this is bad news. When, day in and day out, we sit next to someone who is not living well, then they can stunt our growth. We need to be gently challenged in our friendships. If we surround ourselves with people who we are just our 'public persona' with, we will never be authentic and therefore never be extended. We need to be encouraged to question ourselves and try new ways of being. Growth, not stagnation.

Drinking with buddies can become your lifestyle when you regularly disappear from life with alcohol together. The danger here is that you are not letting yourself sit in your actual loneliness, and so you don't become motivated to form meaningful, intimate friendships that will enable you to grow – the sort that do not rely on alcohol. For people who stay in 'drinking buddies' mode, it is like treading water in life; years pass without growth. Each person normalises the others' daily routine of meeting, drinking and having only light conversation. This is not a deep connection or friendship; this is just socialising with alcohol. This is just passing time.

One profound gift of friendships is wonderful conversations that are both engrossing and exhilarating. This is not just about having interesting thoughts, humour and facts to share; this is about being intrigued by how our friend thinks and approaches things, learning about their views and experiences. The closeness of the conversation, our rambling together, is more important than sharing profound content.

It is through intimate friendships that we experience life intensely. Friendships provide us with an opportunity to find new challenges through each other's company. This becomes fertile grounding for us to experience a **state of flow** – a state of being absorbed in and energised by a meaningful activity, as described in detail in Book 3. Through learning more and more about our friend's individuality and their approach to their world, we can discover more about ourselves as individuals. They broaden our experience and exposure to the world. One of the incredible benefits of my work is the exposure I have to thousands of peoples' worlds. They intrigue and inspire my passion for living as I am stimulated by their worlds and their knowledge base.

In friendship, the key is listening to each other. Having an open, curious and caring mind towards each other. Time with friends is a special opportunity to express private parts of yourself. We are honoured to be invited into each other's personal lives, so we need to listen, concentrate and be sensitive to each other's world. And of course, you usually get back what you give.

Friendship is about being ourselves, letting our hair down and not being on duty. Friendship can help us experience the freedom of the self. With this freedom we can continue to learn and form who we are. This extends to marriage;

ideally our best friend is our spouse. This means we are with the person who we most prefer to spend time with. No matter how passionate our romances, they will eventually wither if the passion is not accompanied by deep friendship.

CHAPTER 26
MALE AND FEMALE FRIENDSHIPS – DIFFERENT PATHWAYS

Generally speaking, there are vast differences in how male and female friendships work. I am talking about how men spend time together, and how women spend time together.

Women tend to 'be', and men tend to 'do' when it comes to friendships. Women can become friends over meeting for a coffee and a chat. Many women form a community together. Men, however, tend to need to become friends over *doing* something together, and then to keep catching up over doing the shared interest together. This might be golf, watching a sport, fishing or fixing something. Basically, if they are grabbing their tools and heading out to hunt together like their forefathers, they are happy. They can put their primary focus on the doing of the activity, not on the building of conversation, their intimacy or their friendship. Woman, on the other hand, meet to unashamedly create their friendship, to connect and build a bridge of familiarity. These are generalisations, and there are many exceptions, but the pattern is common enough to warrant attention.

What this means is that many women can reach out and create a friendship with a fairly straightforward approach. Men, on the other hand, need a situation to bring them together. Many men are friends with old school mates whose past school situation or shared sport teams brought them together. It is very common for men not to re-friend with new people if they lose contact or grow away from these old friends, though work links can create friendships. This can be very isolating, and many men end up having few friendships. It is also sadly common for men to get lost in their focus on work, and let friendship slide away.

Countless male clients have talked to me about this issue, while women lament that they wish their husband had friendship groups. This is why many men play golf, join motocross, or get involved with their kids' interests on an intense level: they are creating bridges to friendship. The key is to understand how important it is for men to get involved in activities that they can do with other men in order to make and sustain friendships.

Once the friendships are established over time, men often soften and they can just catch up. Here in Australia, it is often over a beer at the pub or a BBQ at home – classic Australian, male behaviour. We also have 'men's shed', a community organisation set up so men can come and tinker in a shed together, use the resources and enjoy each other's company. We need to embrace the differences in gender and be sensitive to what we all need. Then we can set ourselves up to create the friendships we want.

CHAPTER 27
OUR ROLE MODELS, OUR MENTORS

Having a mentor is a wonderful thing. A good mentor is someone who has a good sense of who they are and what they need to make their way in the world. This is someone you can trust to be of good will and generous in spirit. Our role models show us a way to see our potential; they plant the seed of aspiration. We need to be like bowerbirds, collecting inspiration from people doing interesting work, and having interesting hobbies, conversations and insights. We can happily be influenced by anyone who inspires or fuels our sense of imagination and purpose. It is great to read autobiographies of inspirational characters and see what you relate to, what jumps out as their strengths that you want to emulate, what ideas you can learn from them to make it through the world.

We need to embrace positive influence. We are a mash-up of what we choose to let into our life. And we are largely a sum of these influences: family, friends, social media, books, films, music, our online activity, our community. As the German writer Goethe said, 'We are shaped and fashioned by what we love', so we have to be careful about what shapes us. Clearly the shallow and corrupting forces of advertising and social media are hard at work trying to shape us. Role models and mentors are our way of actively deciding what positive forces we are going to bring into our lives.

You can pick and choose who will inspire your world. They will shape you; they will guide your view of how to approach your day and how to treat people, and they will influence your outlook on life – all of which can inspire your ambitions in life. It is inspiring being with those who know more than you. Seeking a role model means finding someone to extend you, to push you in a good direction. We all need teachers in our lives, and we always keep our teachers with us in the way that we have been shaped – our thoughts, attitudes and life skills. We internalise their influence.

> *Find the most talented person in the room,*
> *and if it's not you, go stand next to him.*
> *Hang out with him. Try to be helpful.*
> Harold Ramis, actor

> ... and *If you ever find that you're the most talented*
> *person in the room, you need to find another room.*
> – from *Steal like an artist* by Austin Kleon, writer

It can be wonderful for a woman to have access to a powerful, sparky adult woman. Such female role models can ignite strengths in a young woman, strengths that she does not even know she has. These women bring energy to the room; they are grounded and consumed by their own passions in life. They are not trying to influence others and probably have no awareness of the effect they have on others, because that is not their focus. They are just doing their own thing: growing from passion to passion. The pressure on a young woman to conform and fit in with society can pressure her to focus on her similarities with others. This can bury her own uniqueness. The sparky adult woman pulls back this oppressive blanket and can inspire and strengthen her to dance her own dance.

Elderhood is a term used to describe the state of those elders who are deeply and passionately in love with life and with succeeding generations. They have learnt over their many years that generosity, compassion, gentleness and caring are so much more powerful and useful than other ways of being. I am struck by the liberated elderly who carry themselves with such ease in what they say and do. They have learnt to see through society's riddles, superficialities and distractions. In the traditional village, it was understood that elders are no longer physically fit enough to do strenuous things, but they were looked up to because they were seen as the repositories of experience and wisdom, which they could share with the succeeding generations. This is still fortunately the case in many Indigenous communities.

When you work with people who are at the very endpoint of life, you spend time with people who have clarity. I'm talking about those who are on their way to what we clinically call a 'good death' – a death that comes with a sense of contentment about their travels in life. Spending time with people at this endpoint is an honour. This is rare exposure to the true scope of the human condition. I sit there with my ears and heart open to receive their wisdom. I have absolutely taken their wisdom on board and it has fuelled my life direction, my energy and my life passion enormously.

I am going to share with you their truths that I have heard over the last twenty years. The themes are clear. Let's learn from our forefathers and foremothers. Let's listen to their truths. These values resonate with the goal of this book: 'signposts for living'.

WHAT MATTERS:

1. Being proud of their values, fundamentally treating others well, caring for good character and being caring towards others, their family, the courage to travel the world despite the odds, the capacity to give their children a lifestyle they themselves did not have growing up.

2. Having intense pride in their capacity to care for their bodies, to maintain the machine that has got them

through their long lives. Many stories and tricks of the trade for living long and strong (I always listen closely here!). There is not vanity in the care of their bodies, but there is pride in their presentation. There is a contentment in their capacity for self-care of their body, and gentle respect that their bodies can't go on forever.

3. Treasuring their homes, their nests. The place where they have an expression of themselves and they feel safe and content. This secure base is extremely important to them and has become perhaps like another family member. Their home is part of their story.

4. Truly loving others – family, children, pets. Their focal point is time with these loved ones. I state family not generally, but family with whom they have a loving relationship. In fact, non-loving family fade from their focus almost completely. In direct connection with this sincere valuing of love is a decision to not put up with any rot. Any family members who are carrying on in a negative way are not tolerated. They can see that this is just drama fuelled and does not align with their values. They do not usually put up with it, and speak concisely about not wasting their precious time in tolerating it. I recall one woman whose family were busy judging one another for making life choices. The beautiful lady wouldn't even enter into conversation on this point; she just flicked it away like a feather.

5. Experiencing passion. They have conversations on areas of passion and there's no room for chit chat. They want to talk about their hobbies, interests, their family's pursuits, their community's goings-on, world news that interests them, people they are meeting in their week. There is a depth of sincerity in their interest.

6. And finally, not wasting time. I once had a lovely old man say, 'Don't f### around.' He was saying, *Don't waste time, just get in there, live well, live vibrantly.* This has stayed with me and I have lived by this motto ever since. The theme is to create your own life, not a life that society says you should or according to other's expectations of you. Living with vibrancy and honesty is living well.

CHAPTER 28
OTHERS ARE GENEROUS

People are generous. Not always, but mostly. It is important to keep your eye on the fact that in the ordinary world, generosity overpowers greed. People are by their natures wonderfully generous. In our depressive, anxious, self-focused headspaces, we can sometimes lose sight of this.

Of course, when we are happy, we are less self-focused. When we are happy, we want to share our joy and good fortune with others, even strangers. When we are down, however, we turn inward and we focus on our own needs, becoming defensive and distrustful. When we are only looking out for ourselves this shows sadness, not well-being. So it is hard to be generous towards others during these darker patches. But it is during these dark times that awareness of the generosity of others can actually give us a hand to reach for to help us through our personal sludge. The generosity of others is a positive resource surrounding us; see it, celebrate it, reach for it to help us through.

This is the world's wisdom. The world teaches you this: that humans have an infinite capacity to be generous. While there may be dangerous and awful people, they are by far the minority, so let's not tar the rest of the population with their brush. In line with your own wisdom be kind, joyous and patient with others. Others will recognise the same in you. Then we will have the beautiful contagious ripple effect: kindness builds on kindness. As I've suggested before, the energy and attitude you put out comes back to you.

I see this at work all the time; people come in all stony and prickly, with defences full of bravado, and I am relaxed, kind and a bit goofy with them. They drop their defences and then we are just two, kind, simple beings talking to each other. They feel safe. The shared generosity shines. Look to the generosity in people and be one of these generous people. If you are kind and generous, it works better for you in the end. It is a better journey.

CHAPTER 29
SERVE OTHERS, OUR TRIBE, OUR COMMUNITY

There is no doubt, wanting good for others is the unfailing recipe for our own happiness. Good people do things for other people. Happiness is so amazing that it doesn't matter if it is yours or someone else's. We find meaning in devoting ourselves to others and to our community, in loving others and in creating things that give us meaning and purpose. It is about having an ever-greater connection with others and to our world, our community, our society, our moral core. We used to be aware only of our immediate village; now we have the world's affairs at our doorstep. Having goodwill towards others softens our heart. It moves aside separateness and prejudice. It involves compassion, equanimity, reconciliation, joy and connection.

There is a growing body of research that shows that connectedness, meaningful relationships and living with a sense of purpose are vital for our physical health and wellbeing; having these things helps us live longer and have more resilience from illness. When we give back to our community, we are creating a small world of those we love and who love us. This is one of the deepest and most satisfying qualities of well-being.

Our society is slowly waking up to this truth. There is a movement from individualism to community, from competitiveness to collaboration and from status to connection. Instead of taking, we are turning towards the power and purpose of giving.

> *Giving and sharing and gentility and graciousness are not signs of weakness, they're signs of strength.*
> David Amram, composer

Are *you* giving to your community? It really gives us enormous satisfaction to offer others what we have to give: our time, our expertise, our ear, our care or our storytelling. This is not about giving money; this is the giving of ourselves and watching something meaningful being built. This is about sharing companionship and effort. It is not about having impressive skills. It is just about getting involved.

We get respect from others when we offer help. Many people are lonely, and they need someone to pitch in next to them, or just share their company. You do not need to look far to see ways to become involved: schools, retirement villages, hospitals, shelters, community events or church. There are numerous organisations that are working to make the world a better place and to help others, so choose one. Don't assume that it is too late to get involved. Reach out with your time and care, and because you are needed, you will find new respect for yourself. This includes random acts of kindness: picking up litter, being kind to a stranger, showing warmth in your daily interactions. You will feel the warm feeling inside, the sweetness of connecting with others and the world.

This is also an avenue to get more of what you want in life. When we give to other people what we would really like for ourselves, it comes back to us. If you want more love in your life, the clear way to make this happen is to be more loving to others. If you want more playfulness and lightness, then you need to be more playful towards others. Start the dance. This is a profound life realisation to have and skill to nurture.

When we are less self-focused, we are happier. And when we are happier, we are less self-focused. There is something to this. Our community, our people, our world can strangely be our antidote to our own undoing. When we are down, we turn inward; we become distrustful and focus on our own needs, and we become defensive. We begin to look out only for ourselves. When we are happy, we actually like others more. We become less self-focused and more generous towards others. Reaching out to our community can start this cycle of getting out of our own way and becoming other-person orientated. Again, this comes back to the simple power of being kind to others.

However, there is a proviso. This giving to the community has to be with boundaries and self-care. There is no room for martyrdom, where you give to the detriment of yourself. There needs to be balance and a sustainable approach. You have a duty of care to look after yourself first. You can only help others in a healthy way if you have your own balance of self-care on track. You need to tune into your energy reserves. That is *your* responsibility – no one else's – and you have to take this very seriously. If you keep yourself healthy, then you can help others be healthy.

We as human beings are part of the whole. We think we are separate from others in our thoughts, feelings and our experiences, but this is an illusion. We become restricted by our personal desires and tend to reach only for people nearest to us. But we need to realise that we are all connected. Albert Einstein was passionate about this reality. He wrote once in a letter that we are able to 'free ourselves ... by widening our circle of compassion to embrace all living creatures and the whole of nature in its beauty.'

IN CONCLUSION

'Signposts for Living' is about how life is not linear; it is messy. This is especially the case when it comes to our people. To live a good life we must understand how to create our own inner strength from the inside out. Our relationships and our interpersonal reactions to others are fertile ground for this learning. Living well means opening our heart to what our inner workings and the world can show us. Sometimes it is terrifying and sometimes it is beautiful. Take both. It is our human right to be treated with respect and to be safe with others. It is our human need to feel understood and to feel cared for and prioritised by our loved ones. But it is equally our responsibility to do no harm to others and to love and nurture them in return. This treaty goes both ways. Take pride in your standards for how you love others, and how you equally love yourself, expecting only the best for all.

FURTHER READING

John O'Donohue offers poignant observations in his prose, and John Gottman provides a wonderful resource for couples wanting to navigate the common challenges faced in the various stages of relationships. You might like to explore some of their works, listed below.

Gottman, J (2018), *The seven principles for making marriage work*, Orion Publishing Co, London.

O'Donohue, J (2000), *Eternal echoes: exploring our hunger to belong*, Harper Collins, New York.

O'Donohue, J (2008), *To bless the space between us: a book of blessings*, Doubleday, New York.

And, finally, if you wish to explore the topics I have touched on briefly in this book more deeply, you might like to try the other books in the 'Signposts for Living' series by Dr Kirsten Hunter:

Book 1: Control your Consciousness – In the Driver's Seat

Book 2: Understanding Myself – Be an Expert

Book 3: Mindfulness and State of Flow – Living with Purpose and Passion

Book 5: Parenting – Love, Pride, Apprenticeship

Book 6: Nailing Being an Adult – Have the Skills

ACKNOWLEDGEMENTS

To Jon, my beautiful husband, your support is constant. I can always rely on you to be in my corner, patiently championing me on while I sit typing away. With writing, having someone who believes in you makes all the difference. Thank you that it is always 'us' facing the next challenge, the next hurdle. I love you.

My devoted mum has been the rock through my childhood and every chapter of my adulthood. No child could have a more extraordinary mum. I'm proud of you and I love you.

Our five boys, Lachlan, James, Tobias, Jack, and George, when you heard that your mum was writing books, non-fiction and fiction, your response was simply 'of course she is'. When you heard mum was publishing, your response was 'of course she is'. When we talk about the book being successful in reaching a wide audience, your response, 'of course it will'. You boys are so beautiful. Ever-resounding support, thank you. I love you.

Vanya Lowther, you are the smartest person I know, and perhaps the wisest. You are also my closest and my lifelong friend. Thank you for taking on the mammoth task of being the first person to put your eyes on the *Signposts for Living* books. Your perseverance, your contribution and brainpower was and is so appreciated. I love you.

Jane Smith, I agree with Stephen King, 'to write is human, to edit is divine'. Thank you for your eye for detail, your grammatical wizardry and staying fresh when there was so much work to do. You're a talented gem.

ABOUT THE AUTHOR

Dr Kirsten Hunter is a clinical psychologist with 20 years' experience working with children, adolescents, adults, and couples across the expanse of clinical areas. Between running her private practice, enjoying time with her family, and writing her books, Kirsten juggles a range of passions – particularly for scuba diving and hiking. Kirsten is known for diving deep into life, creating and embracing all of life's opportunities. Born in Brisbane, she now lives in Toowoomba, Australia, with her six men: her husband and their five sons. Even their pets are male ...

www.ingramcontent.com/pod-product-compliance
Lightning Source LLC
Chambersburg PA
CBHW041956080526
44588CB00021B/2761